THE CUTEST BEGINNER DRAWING BOOK EVER

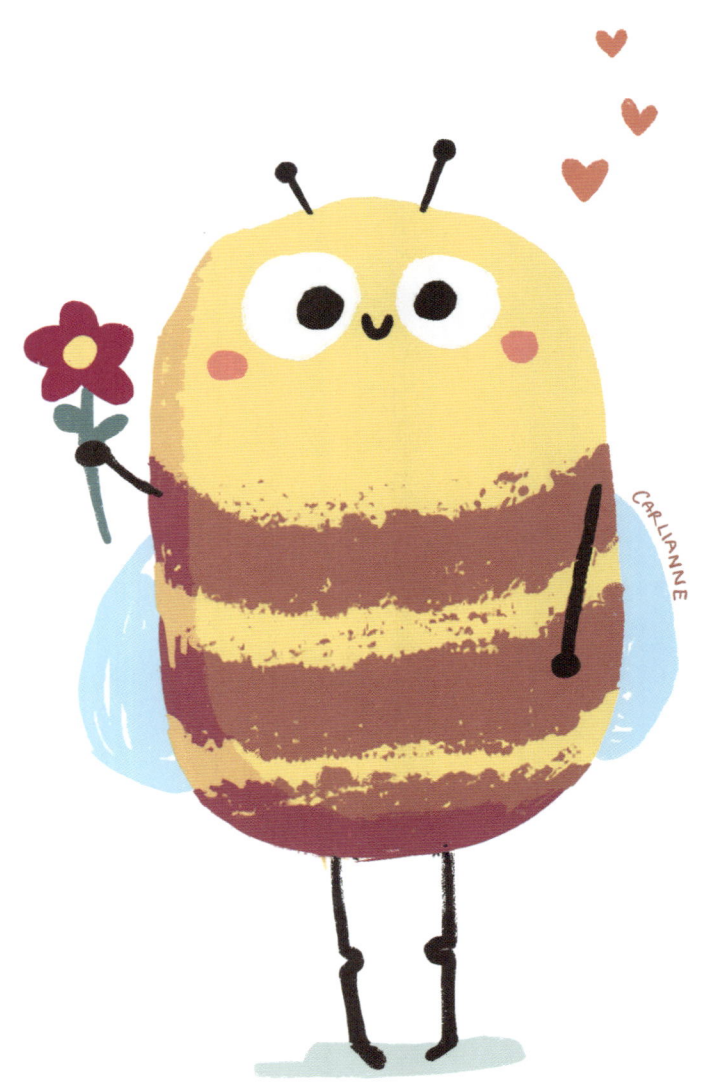

THE CUTEST BEGINNER DRAWING BOOK EVER

BY CARLIANNE TIPSEY

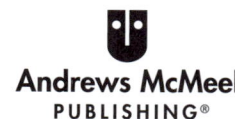

Andrews McMeel
PUBLISHING®

CUTEST BEGINNER DRAWING BOOK EVER copyright © 2025 by Carlianne Tipsey. All rights reserved. Printed in China. No part of this book may be used or reproduced in any manner whatsoever without written permission, except in the case of reprints in the context of reviews.

The authorised representative in the EEA is Simon and Schuster Netherlands BV, Herculesplein 96 3584 AA Utrecht, Netherlands. (info@simonandschuster.nl)

Andrews McMeel Publishing
a division of Andrews McMeel Universal
1130 Walnut Street, Kansas City, Missouri 64106

www.andrewsmcmeel.com

26 27 28 29 30 RLP 10 9 8 7 6 5 4 3 2 1

ISBN: 979-8-8816-0183-6

Editor: Amanda Meadows
Art Director/Designer: Julie Barnes
Production Editor: Julie Railsback
Production Manager: Tamara Haus

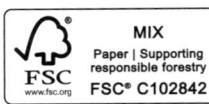

ATTENTION: SCHOOLS AND BUSINESSES
Andrews McMeel books are available at quantity discounts with bulk purchase for educational, business, or sales promotional use. For information, please email the Andrews McMeel Publishing Special Sales Department: sales@andrewsmcmeel.com.

To my friend Simona,
Grazie Infinite

contents

introduction • 9
drawing tools & tips • 13
all about lines • 25
shaping things up • 35
let's add volume • 49
constructing new shapes • 63
just a lil' perspective • 71
let's add value • 93
composing your art • 107
characters anyone can draw • 123
fun with animals • 141
let's celebrate! • 153
glossary of terms • 156
additional resources • 160

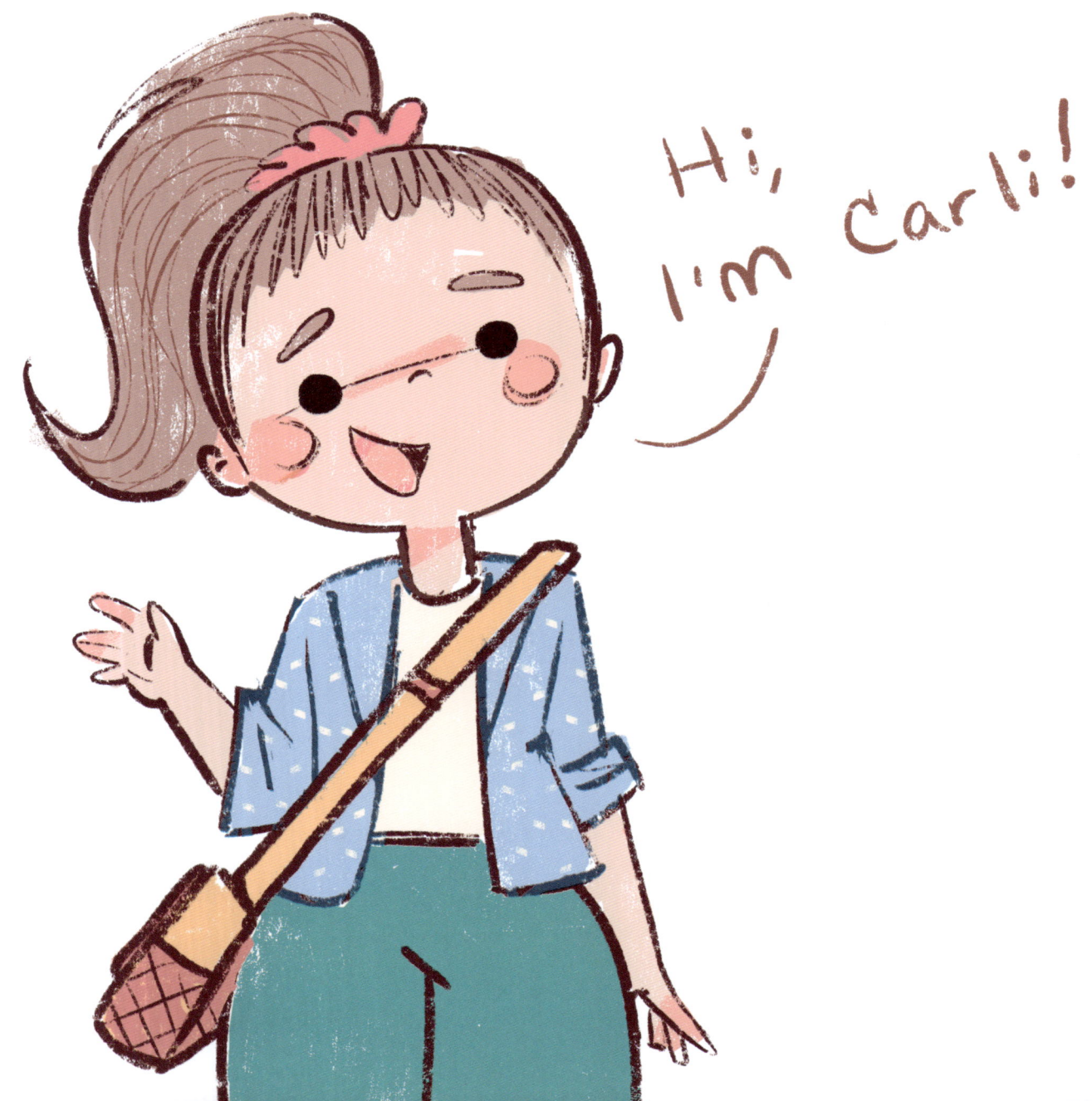

INTRODUCTION

I'M ON A MISSION TO INSPIRE FUTURE ARTISTS WITH SIMPLE AND FUN TUTORIALS.

Hi, my name is Carlianne, and I am the award-winning author/illustrator of *How to Draw Adorable: Joyful Lessons for Making Cute Art*. I started my career working in games for Disney interactive but eventually left to pursue my love of children's illustration. Through out my career I found I had a unique ability to help other artists and began posting simple tutorials on social media. I have been so fortunate for the support on Instagram, TikTok, and YouTube that led me to launching my first book, and now this one! I am a firm believer that learning art can be simple, fun, and easy especially when keeping it simple with adorable art.

So buckle up, because you're about to start drawing some seriously cute stuff.

IF YOU'VE LOST YOUR SPARK

This page is for those of you who started out drawing and somewhere along the line fell out of love or felt their dreams were unachievable.

Whether it's through crayons, markers, or finger painting, the joy found in creating can be seen at all ages. So what causes some of us to consider that they can't create art, aren't good at it, or don't enjoy it anymore?

I have found that many of us got discouraged from making art when we started to get "critiqued" by others (or ourselves) and felt like we didn't measure up. There were too many losses and not enough successes.
As a mom, however, when I look at the art my kids make, I never think, "Oh, their perspective is terrible." I think, "This is so creative and fun!"

This book will help you improve your drawing technique, for sure. But I also hope that you find that learning artistic skills and improving your technique are tools to help you communicate your message better, and are absolutely not a measurement of YOU. And that even a stick figure or a little circle with a smile on it is art!

I encourage you to make mistakes, break the rules, and create art that brings you joy. I'll give you some guideposts to help you so that you're not fumbling your way, but remember these are guides to help you communicate the right message, not to dictate if what you are doing is "good" or "bad."

Because even the most scribbly wonky sketch can be beautiful art.

Carlianne

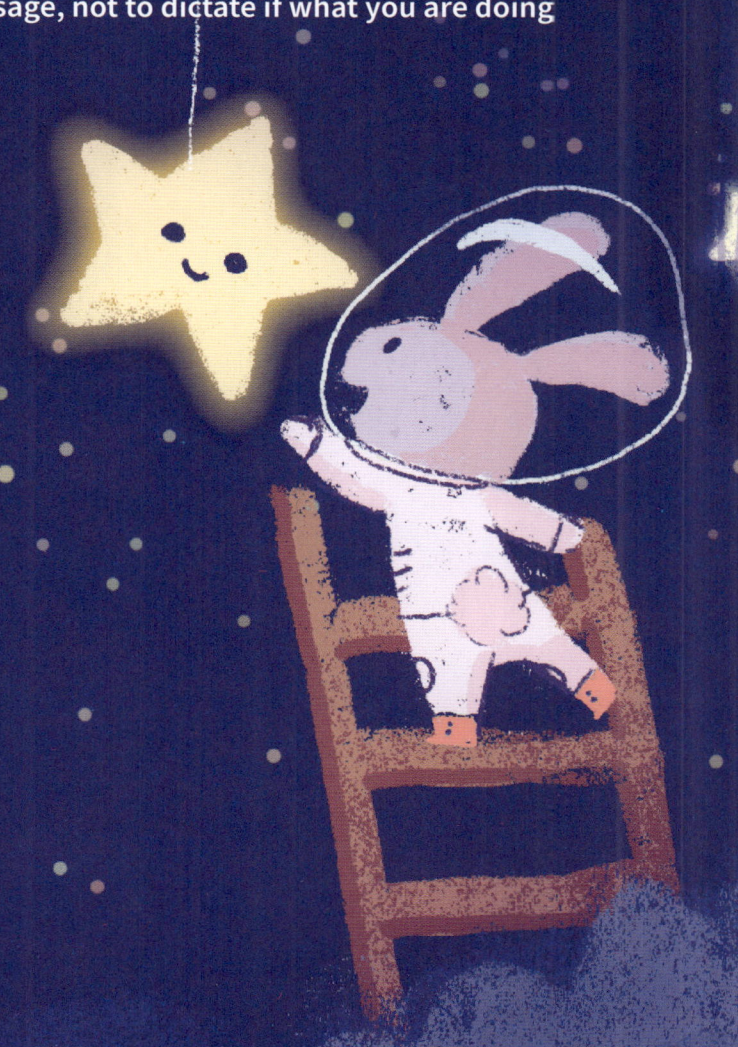

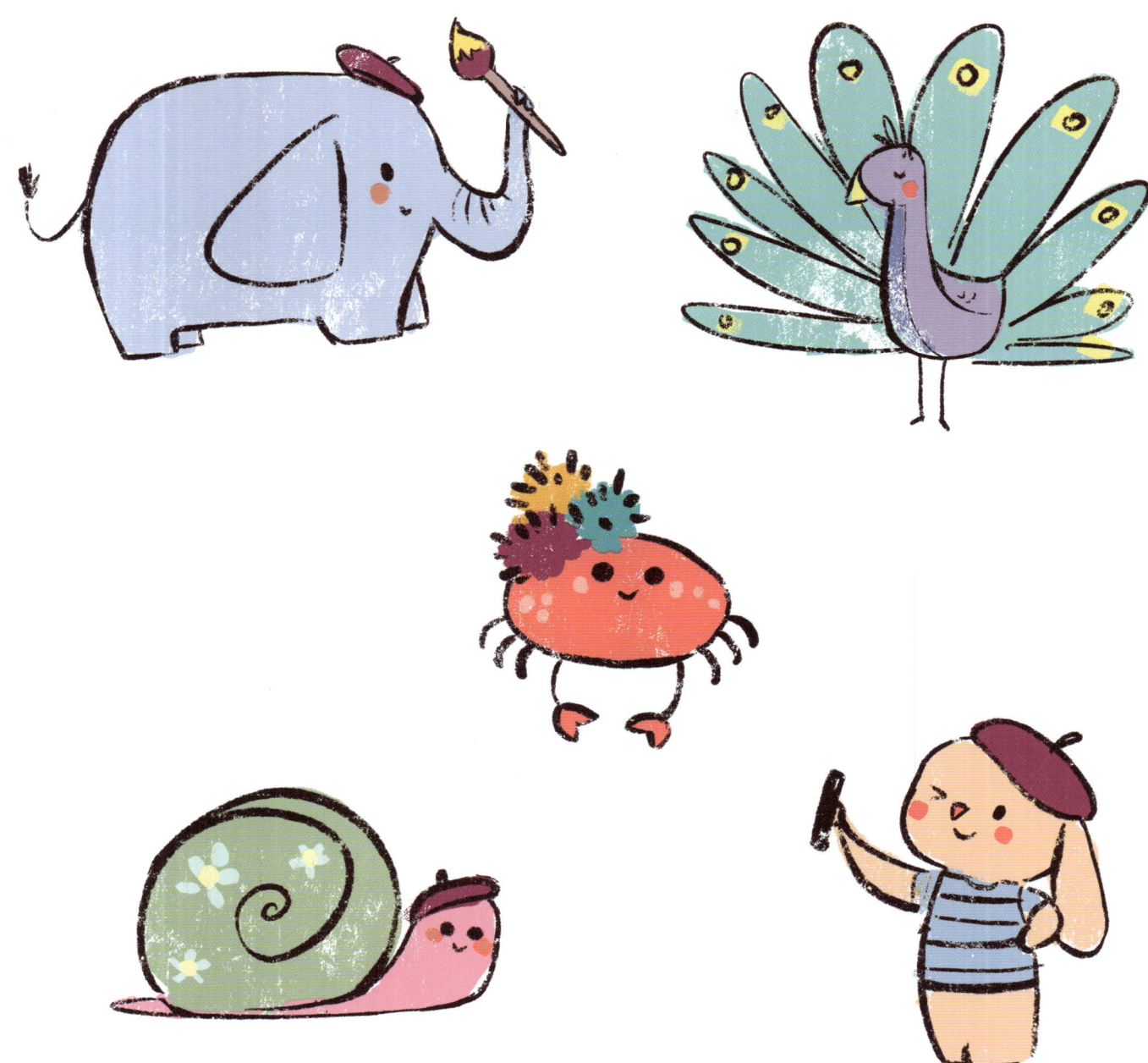

DRAWING TOOLS & TIPS

LEARNING TO DRAW SHOULDN'T FEEL SCARY. Have you ever looked at a drawing book or art tutorial and immediately thought it was so advanced that you didn't even feel like you should try? Me too, and I went through art school and worked professionally for over a decade! I realized that there is actually an easier way to go about learning to draw—and it's more fun, too! I want to break learning to draw down into bite-sized steps so that you can have confidence and pride in your drawings right from the start. Then I'll show you how to practice what you learn so you can get rolling right away. These are not going to be your ordinary drawing assignments. Plus, I'll be giving you frequent tips to make learning more fun!

Ready to start? Let's go!

do your tools matter?

Will getting the right tool make you a better artist? Not really. However, it can make drawing easier, and I like anything that makes your life more easy! Here are a few art tools I like.

MY PENCIL IS A LITTLE SOFTIE

Did you know that some pencils are darker and softer than others? I didn't really know this until art school! Getting a set of pencils that range from 2H (hard and light) to 6B (soft and dark) will be helpful when you do value and shading practice.

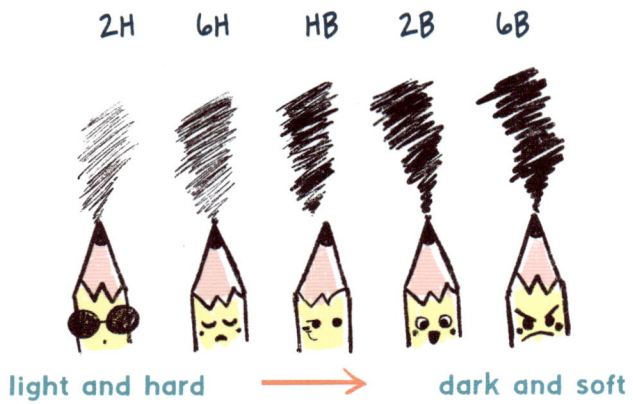

YOU KNEAD . . . THIS ERASER

Aside from a normal eraser you can get a kneaded eraser, too. They feel like putty, don't leave eraser crumbs, and can be used to gently pat the pencil marks away to make the drawing lighter. (Plus they're really fun to mold into silly shapes!)

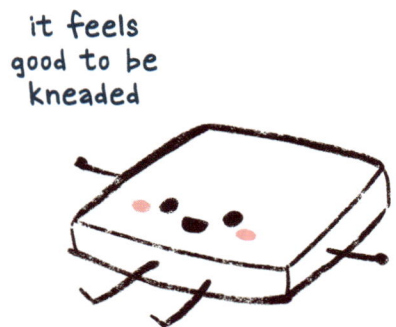

PICK A PAPER

For paper, you'll want a sketchbook (or a drawing pad if you prefer to work really large). You'll need to decide if you prefer to draw on textured paper (hot press) or on smooth paper (cold press). I personally love a textured feel!

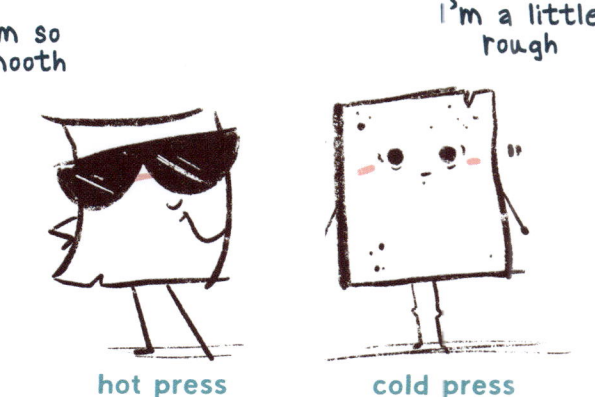

hot press   cold press

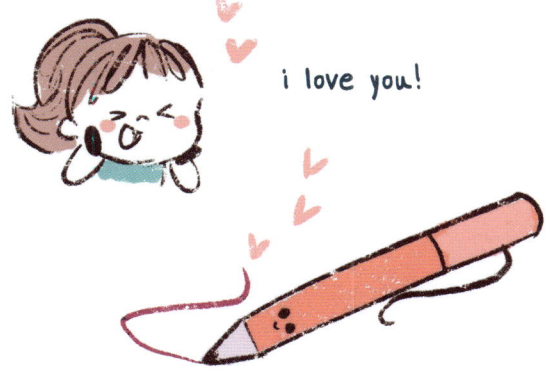

MY PERSONAL SECRET LOVE...

I actually truly love drawing with pen, and use it exclusively in my sketchbook. For me, drawing with pen frees me from attempting to fix my art or erase and allows me to experiment and explore without editing.

YOU MIGHT WANT A BLENDING TOOL

When we get to shadow and light, you might want to try a style where you blend the shadow shapes. If you're using pencil, I recommend a blending stump. You can use your fingers to blend but I once left pencil fingerprints on my white cat during a drawing session, so I don't recommend it.

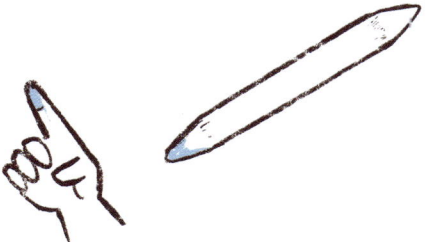

blending tools

DRAWING TOOLS & TIPS

how to learn art

If you've ever wanted to learn about art but didn't know where to start, buckle up while I share the approach I've had toward learning that has helped me become the artist I am today.

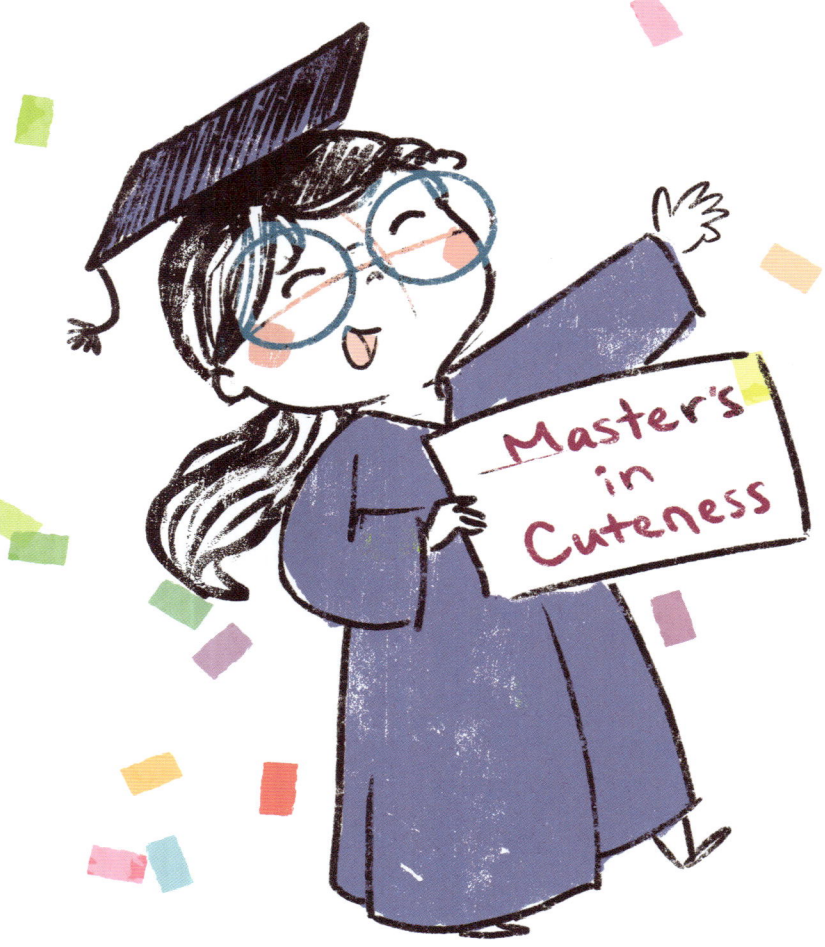

TO IMPROVE AS AN ARTIST YOU NEED TO:

- have a goal in mind
- keep it simple
- practice, practice, practice
- know what you like

let's start right now!

LET'S SET SOME GOALS

By having a goal in mind, you'll have a guidepost to judge whether or not you've actually improved or are making progress towards your goal.

MAYBE YOU'D LIKE TO . . .

improve your doodles

have more confidence

make money with your art

GO AHEAD. DREAM BIG.

I want to be a *New York Times* bestselling author and have a million followers on social media. It's so big, I almost feel silly to say it. But I'll never get it if I don't try. Write your personal goals, big or small in this space right here. You don't have to show anyone. It can be a secret just between you and me.

DRAWING TOOLS & TIPS **17**

ONE STEP AT A TIME

Learning art is like climbing a ladder. If there are steps missing, it'll suddenly seem super hard! For example, drawing in perspective is harder than drawing flat shapes. Putting shadow on a ball is easier than on a face.

IF YOU GET FRUSTRATED

You might not have practiced the easier stuff enough. Go back and do the easier stuff a little more, or try to find a middle step that is missing.

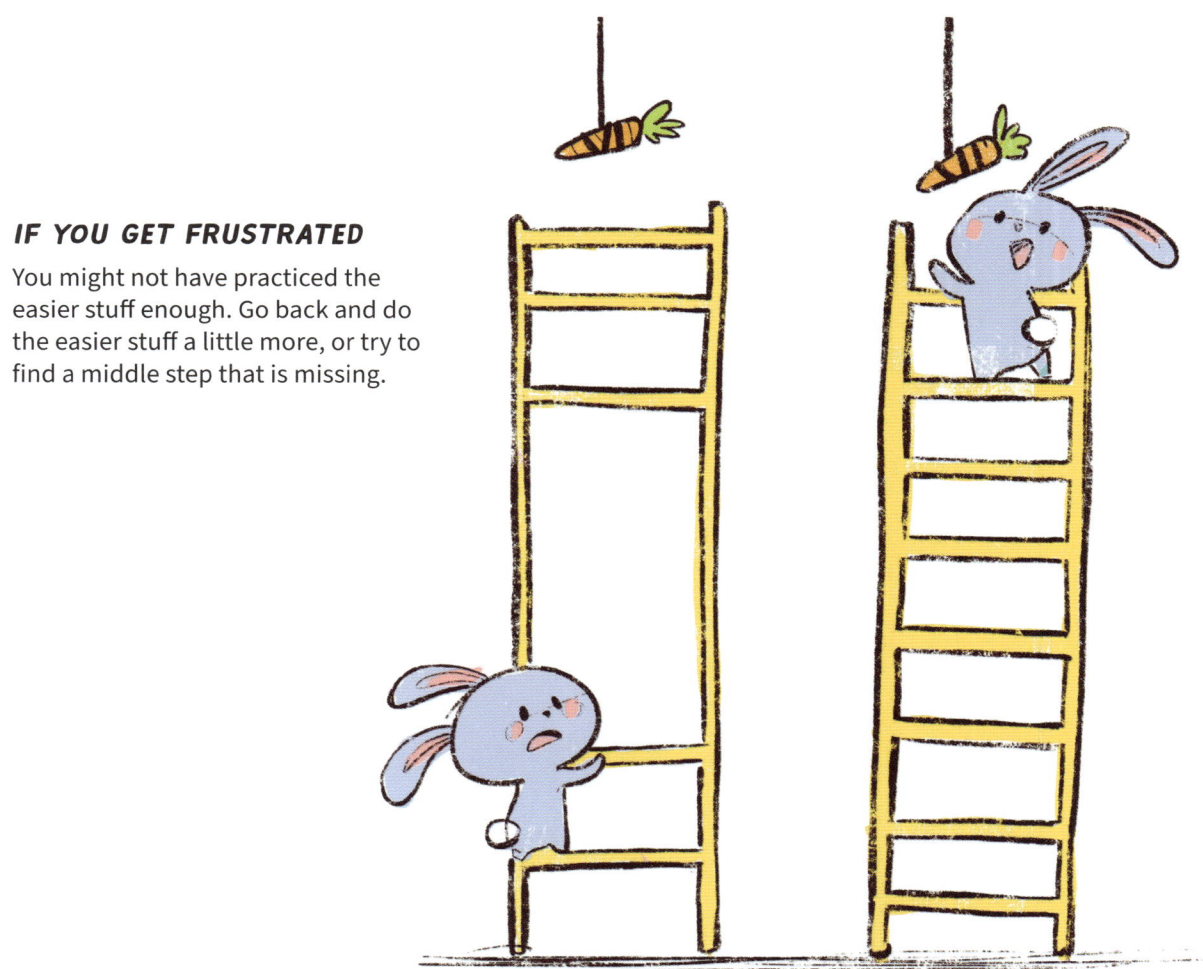

PRACTICE, PRACTICE, PRACTICE

The only way to fail is to not try again. If you don't like what you made, just try it again. Here's some examples from my sketchbook where I was drawing the same character over and over to figure him out.

we love all drawings here

NO SUCH THING AS "BAD DRAWINGS"

I don't believe in bad drawings. But I do have lots of drawings that I've learned from. They aren't bad because they helped me become the artist I am today.

DRAWING TOOLS & TIPS

i love ugly sketches

There, I said it! Down with pretty sketchbooks! A sketch is a rough or unfinished drawing. The purpose of a sketch is to learn, not to make something beautiful to share. If you're not able to sketch because you're trying to make something perfect, then you'll also struggle to explore new ideas and concepts and might slow your growth as an artist.

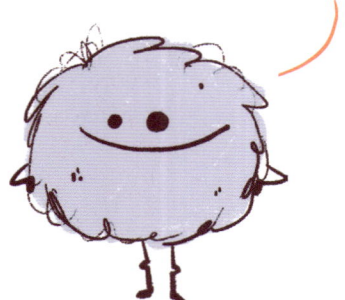

imperfections are welcome here

MY SKETCHY PROCESS

I spend as much time as I can in the sketch stage to work out all the kinks. Plus sketches seem to always have more energy than clean drawings, so by keeping my lines sketchy while I clean it up I am able to keep that extra "life" in my final drawing.

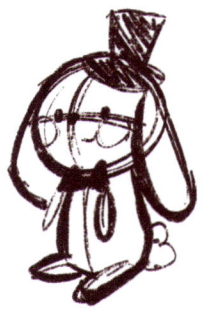
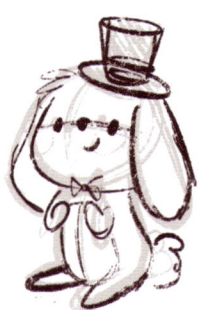
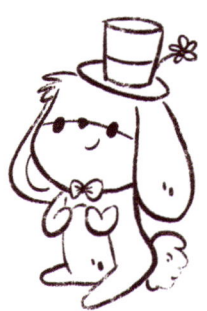
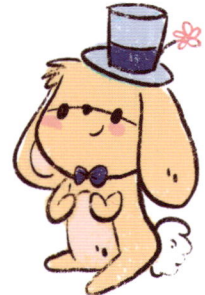

wonky sketch   rough sketch   kinda clean   clean drawing

keep it simple, silly

I think about drawing like building a house. The shakier the foundation, the harder time you'll have building the walls. So I take my time at the early stages of sketching, creating ideas and making decisions before rushing to the final. Here's some examples of that in action.

BIG SHAPES FIRST

When you begin drawing, try starting with the biggest shapes you see first, then clean that up before adding details.

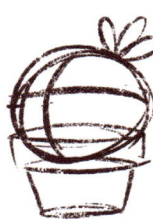 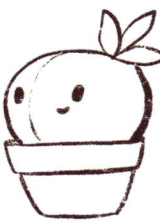 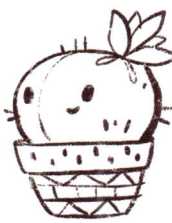

big shapes   **clean up**   **details**

SIMPLE TO COMPLEX

I think about simple to complex in all stages of my art. Whether I'm doing color or looking at the overall composition.

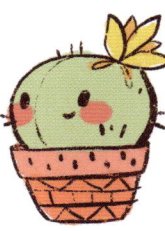 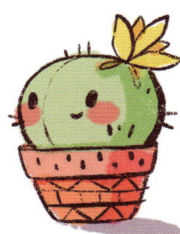 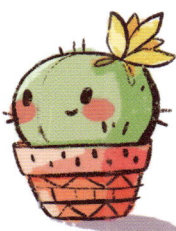

flat color   **light**   **details**

⟨tip!⟩

When you're sketching, try to draw the stuff you won't see, too! This helps you line everything up correctly. For example, I drew the back of the pot and the entire cactus, even though I was planning to erase it later.

draw with x-ray vision

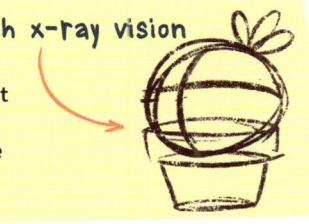

DRAWING TOOLS & TIPS

PRACTICE TIME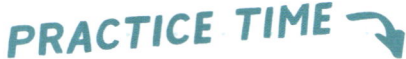

DRAW WHATEVER YOU WANT HERE.

AT THE END OF THE BOOK WE WILL SEE HOW MUCH YOU'VE GROWN.

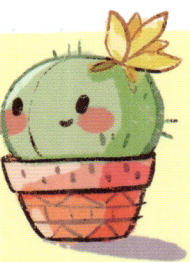

⋛tip!⋚

Can't think of anything to draw? Here are some ideas!

A cat, a tree, a monster, an apple, a silly face, a person dancing, a birthday present, or a donut.

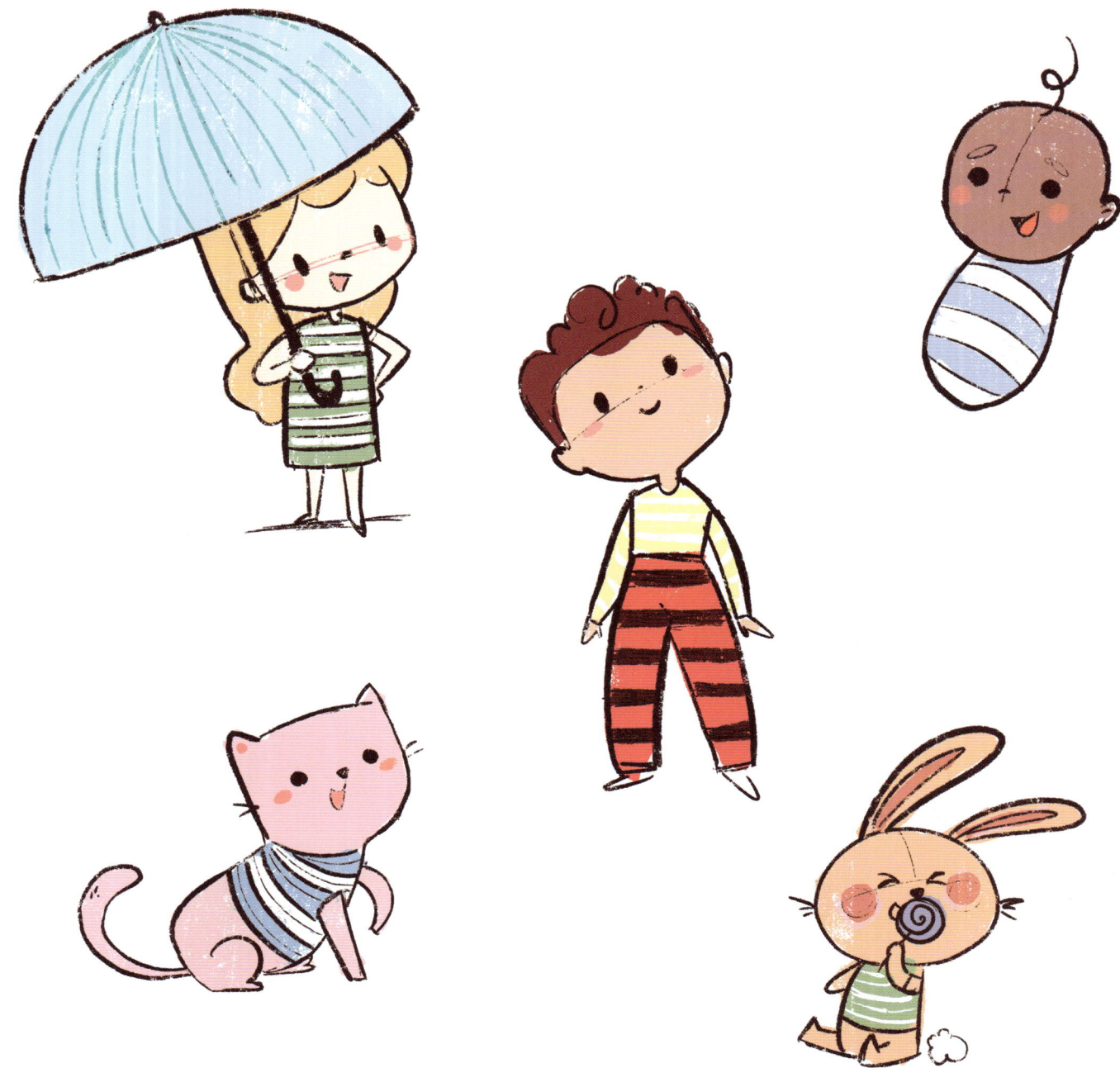

ALL ABOUT LINES

HAVE YOU EVER TRIED TO DRAW AND GOTTEN FRUSTRATED YOUR HAND WASN'T DOING WHAT YOU TOLD IT TO? YEAH, ME TOO!

I felt this way for YEARS until I finally started to do some of the exercises I will show you in this book. It turns out that feeling of frustration is caused by a lack of muscle memory. To fix this, you just have to practice drawing lots of lines and shapes. That way your mind isn't trying to think about each and every mark you're making on the paper and can start to think about the big picture . . . whatever it is you're trying to draw!

Oh, and did I mention this major BONUS? As you begin to draw each line more smoothly and easily, I'm sure you'll see your confidence grow, too.

So come on and let's draw some lines together!

confident line drawings

One of the tricky parts of learning to draw is just figuring out how to get your pencil to do what you want it to! Here are my tips for more confident line drawings.

DRAW LIGHTLY

If you don't press down too hard, there's less friction between your pencil and paper—so your lines end up looking more smooth and confident.

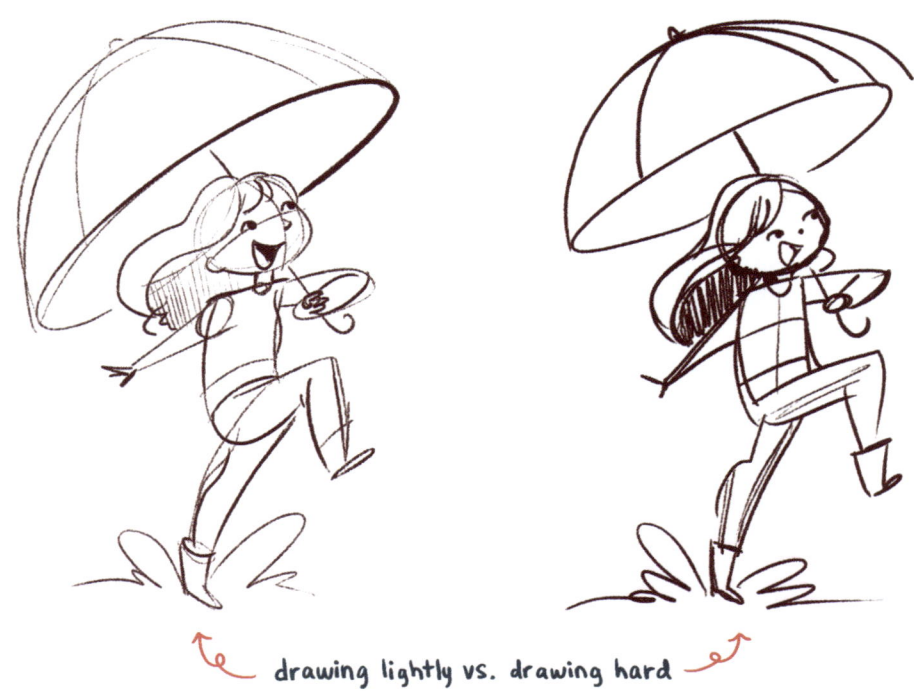

drawing lightly vs. drawing hard

WATCH YOUR SPEED

Sometimes drawing too slowly can make my lines wobbly, but drawing too fast can make my lines less precise. Every artist has their own sweet spot. Try out different speeds to see what is best for you.

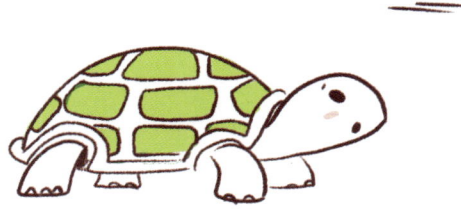

GHOSTING IS OKAY HERE

Have you ever seen a golfer take a swing at a ball? Did you notice they take a few practice swings first? I like to call this motion "ghosting." Ghosting the beginning of the line before putting your pencil to paper helps you draw with more confidence—and make more boo-tiful art.

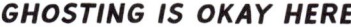

ALL ABOUT LINES **27**

thin vs. thick lines

The final step to total pencil control is being able to control how thin and thick your lines are. This is also known as controlling your line weight.

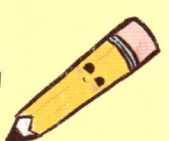

tip!
Most drawing tools can create thick and thin lines, but some pens can make this really tricky. I recommend you grab a pencil to practice this!

CONTROL HOW HARD YOU PRESS DOWN

Pressing lightly usually creates a light line, while pressing harder creates a thicker line. Of course, this does depend a bit upon what you draw with, but most pens and pencils will create this effect!

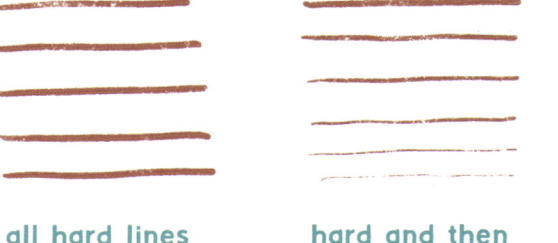

all hard lines   **hard and then light lines**   **gradual change in pressure**

WHICH STYLE DO YOU PREFER?

Using all the same line weight is often used in cartoony styles, and a variety in weight is in more true-to-life styles. Do either of these styles sing to you?

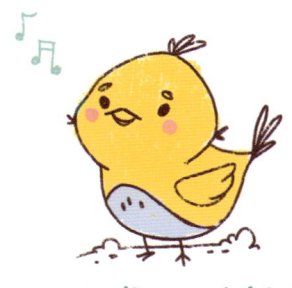
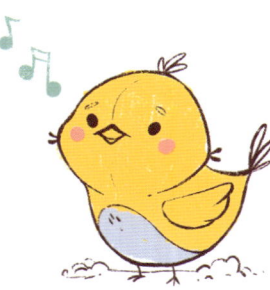

even line weight   **variety in line weight**

WHEN TO DRAW THIN VS. THICK LINES

Controlling when you draw with a thin or thick line in your drawings is a great way to control where a person looks first. Dark and thick lines will pop forward. Thin and light lines will fade away.

CREATE DEPTH

You can even make an object look farther away by using a thinner line! See how the top heart looks farther away than the middle one?

SKETCH LINES FADE

If you draw lightly in your sketch phase, the thicker and darker lines will pop out, and the thin sketch will fade away.

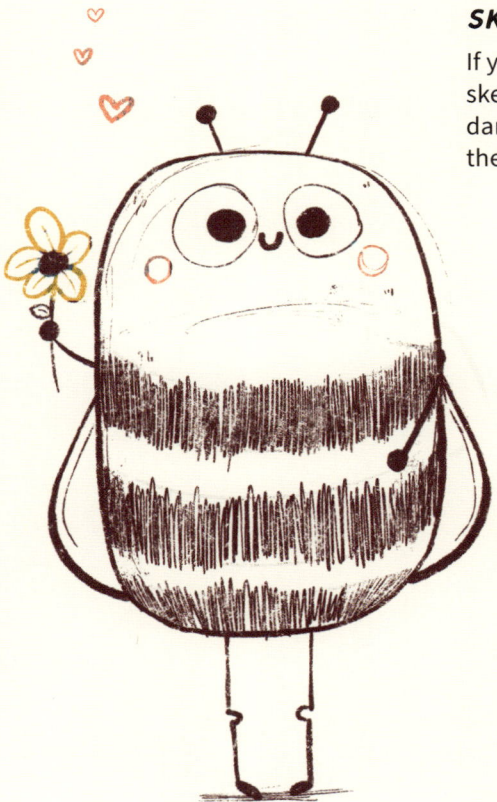

THICK LINES CREATE FOCAL POINTS

The thickest lines in this drawing pop out at you first. For example, the eyes and mouth and flower have the thickest lines in this drawing, so you notice them first.

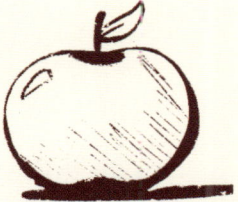

TO CREATE SHADOWS

You can use thin lines on the light side and thicker lines on the dark side to emphasize shadows.

ALL ABOUT LINES

PRACTICE TIME

TRACE THESE STRAIGHT LINES.

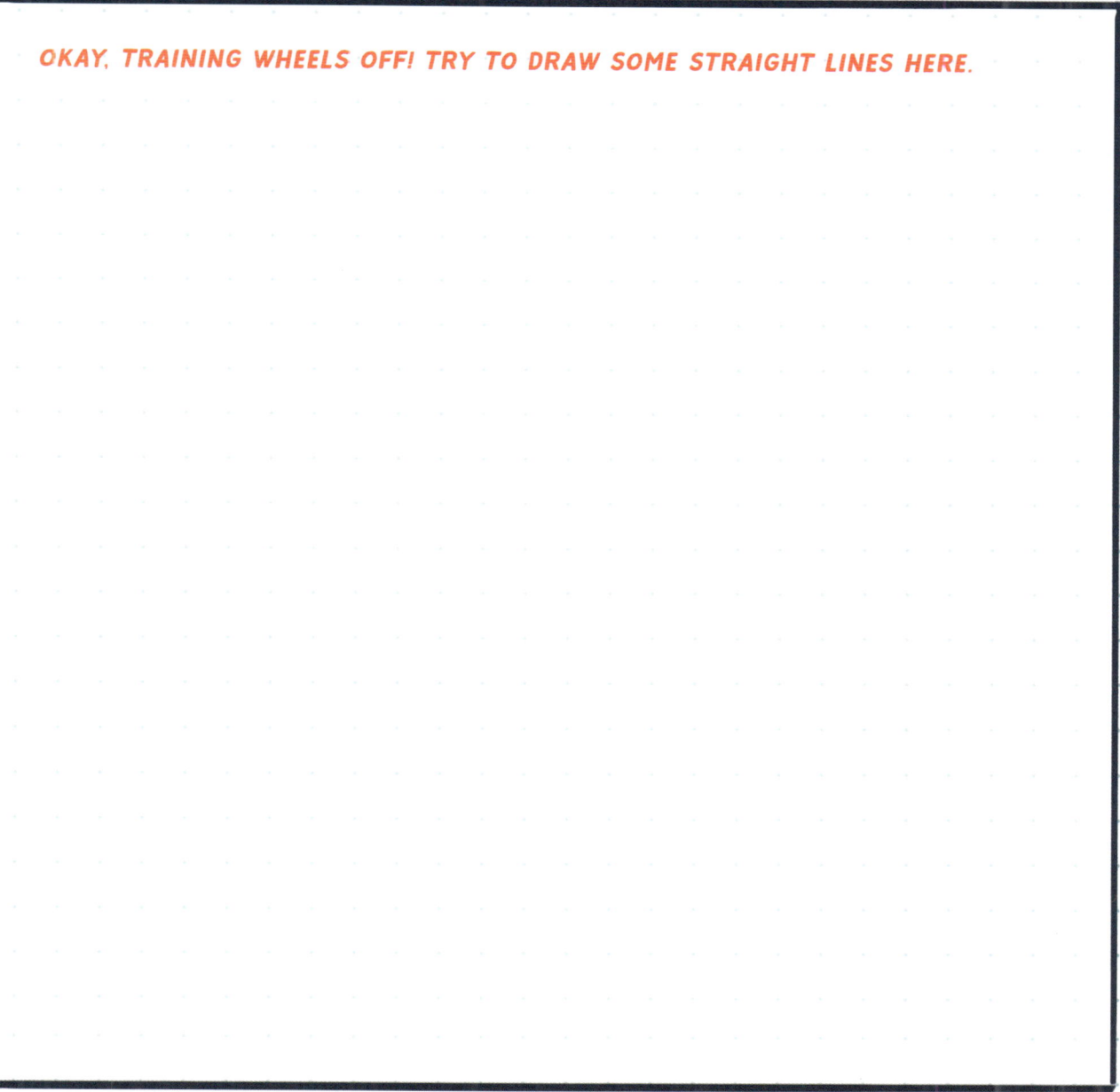

PRACTICE TIME

TRACE THESE PATTERNS LIGHTLY.

DRAW SOME PATTERNS OF YOUR OWN.

ALTERNATE LIGHT AND HEAVY LINES

LIGHT TO HEAVY LINES

LIGHT TO HEAVY AND BACK TO LIGHT LINES

DRAW SOME LINES OF YOUR OWN.

ALL ABOUT LINES **33**

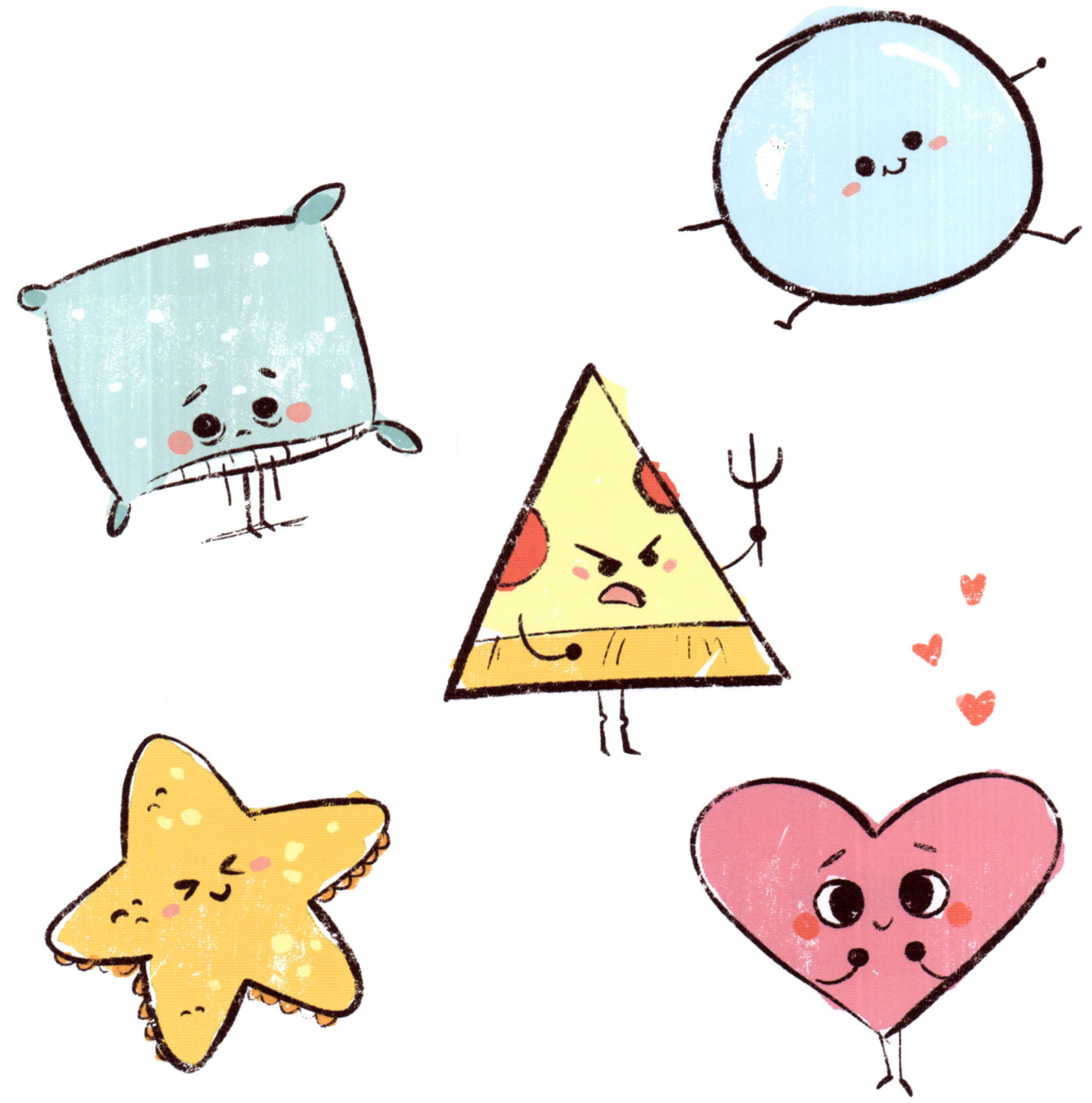

SHAPING THINGS UP

THE KEY TO DRAWING ANYTHING IS IN FINDING THE SIMPLE SHAPES FIRST.

One of the best ways to learn how to draw is by looking at the world around you and learning to draw what you see. The problem is . . . life can seem complicated! I personally always struggled with how to take a complex object or image and find the simple shapes that make it up. The better and more comfortable you are at drawing these shapes, the easier more complex things will be later.

Plus you'll learn about how different shapes have different personalities.

Your drawing is really going to start shaping up here.

shape personality

Wanna know something else fun! These shapes each have their own personalities! Here are the friends we will be working with:

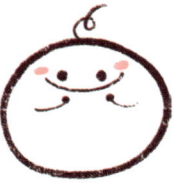

friendly and cute

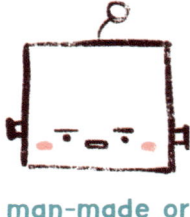

man-made or predictable

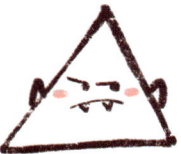

scary or interesting

POINTY OR ROUND SHAPES, TOO

Your shapes don't have to be perfectly round or triangular to have personality. Pointy shapes have the same vibe as triangular shapes, similar with round shapes and circle shapes.

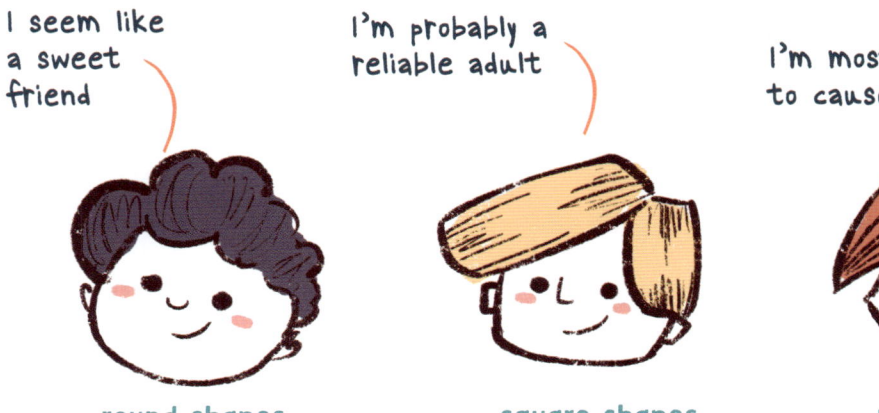

I seem like a sweet friend — round shapes

I'm probably a reliable adult — square shapes

I'm most likely to cause trouble — pointy shapes

draw anything simply

It's easy to draw anything if you're using just simple shapes. Here's an example using the three basic shapes to draw three different kinds of trees!

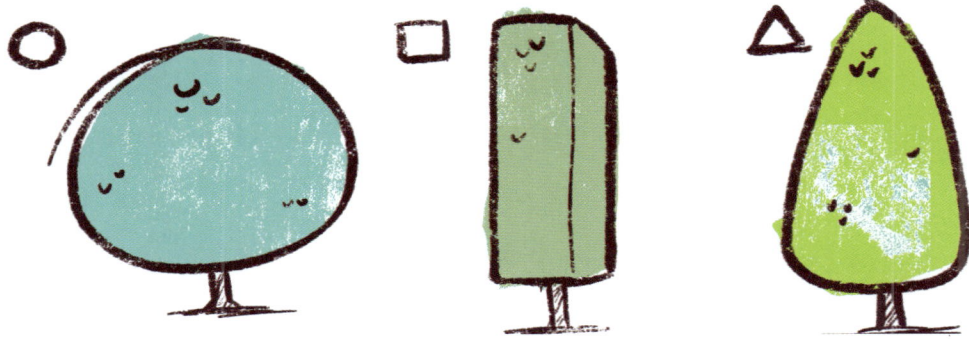

USE SHAPES TO SIMPLIFY

Even when drawing in a more detailed style, you can start with simple shapes to create your sketch and then add details after.

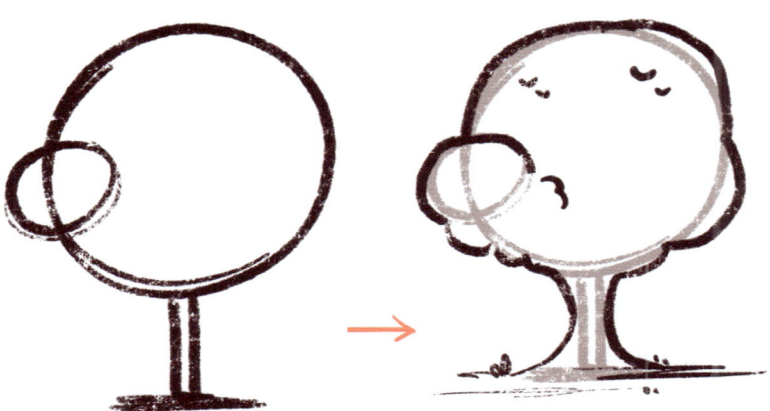

SHAPING THINGS UP 37

ORGANIC SHAPES

You don't have to use perfect circles, triangles, and squares. Any large simple shapes will work, especially with natural items.

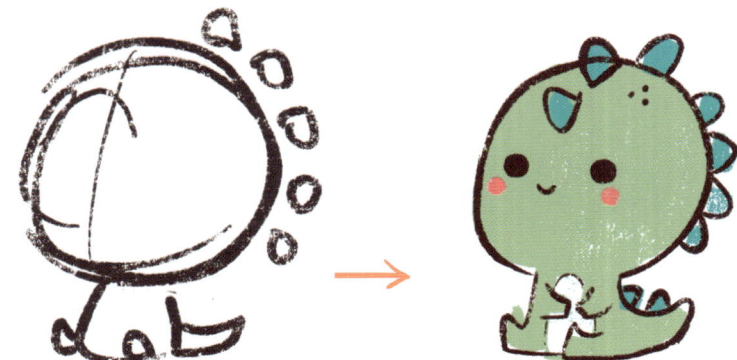

NO WAY TO GO WRONG

I used to think there was a wrong or right way to do this, but it turns out whatever shape you feel makes the most sense is fine! For example, here are two ways you can simplify a hand.

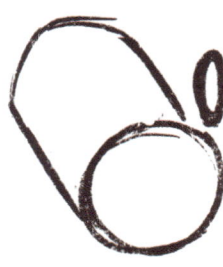

these shapes

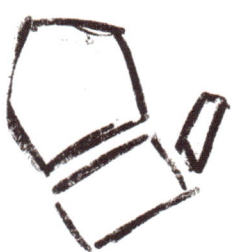

or these shapes

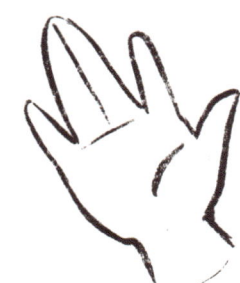

thanks for the hand!

both work to make this

QUICK DRAWING TIPS!

When drawing small circles, you can probably get a good drawing by holding your pencil normally and moving your wrist or fingers. But when you level up to a large circle you'll have more success drawing from your shoulder instead.

> **tip!**
> Remember that drawing lightly to start can also help with this. Sometimes if you're pressing down too hard, your pencil will get kind of stuck on the paper! Yikes!

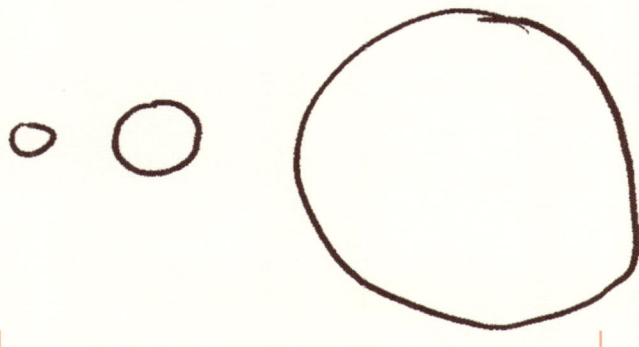

using the wrist

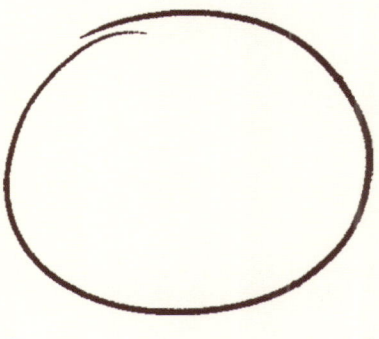

using the shoulder

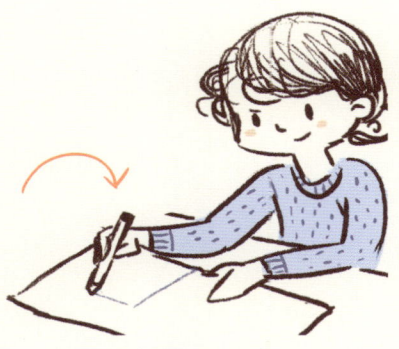

using the wrist

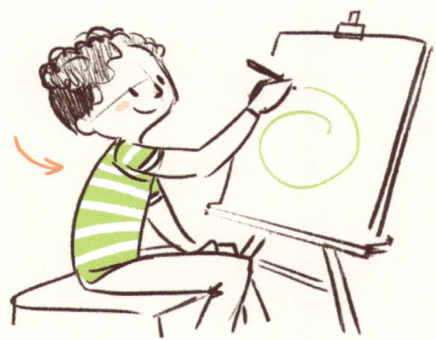

using the shoulder

SHAPING THINGS UP 39

PRACTICE TIME ↪

TRACE THESE CIRCLES.

⁞make it fun!⁞
You can add a face, a pattern, or other details to turn these boring circles into fun doodles! Here are some ideas to get you started.

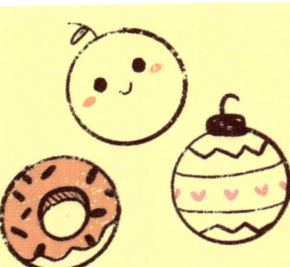

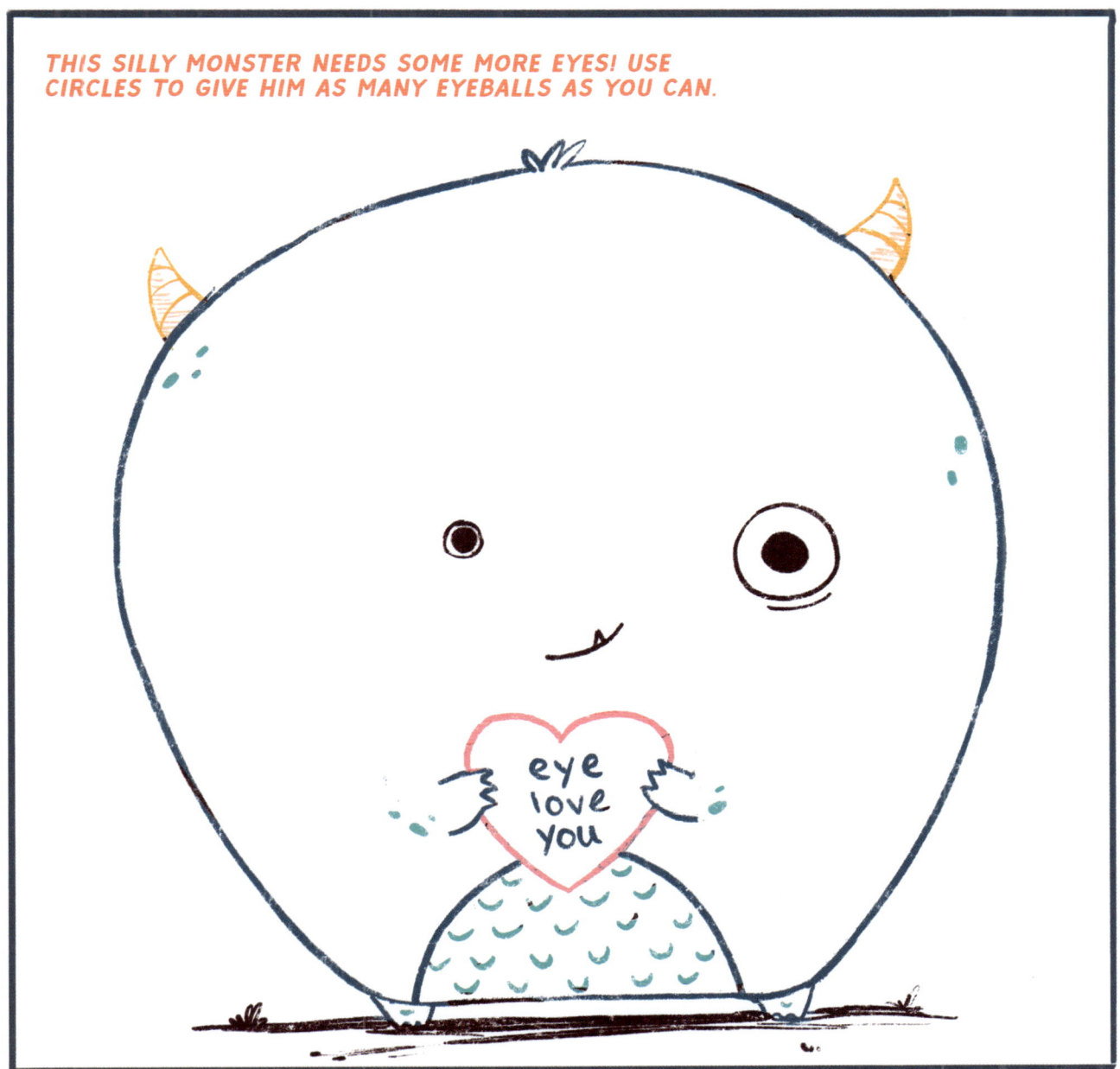

PRACTICE TIME → TRACE THESE SQUARES.

make it fun!
Turn these squares into silly objects or characters! Add a face or other details as you see fit. Here are some ideas to get you started.

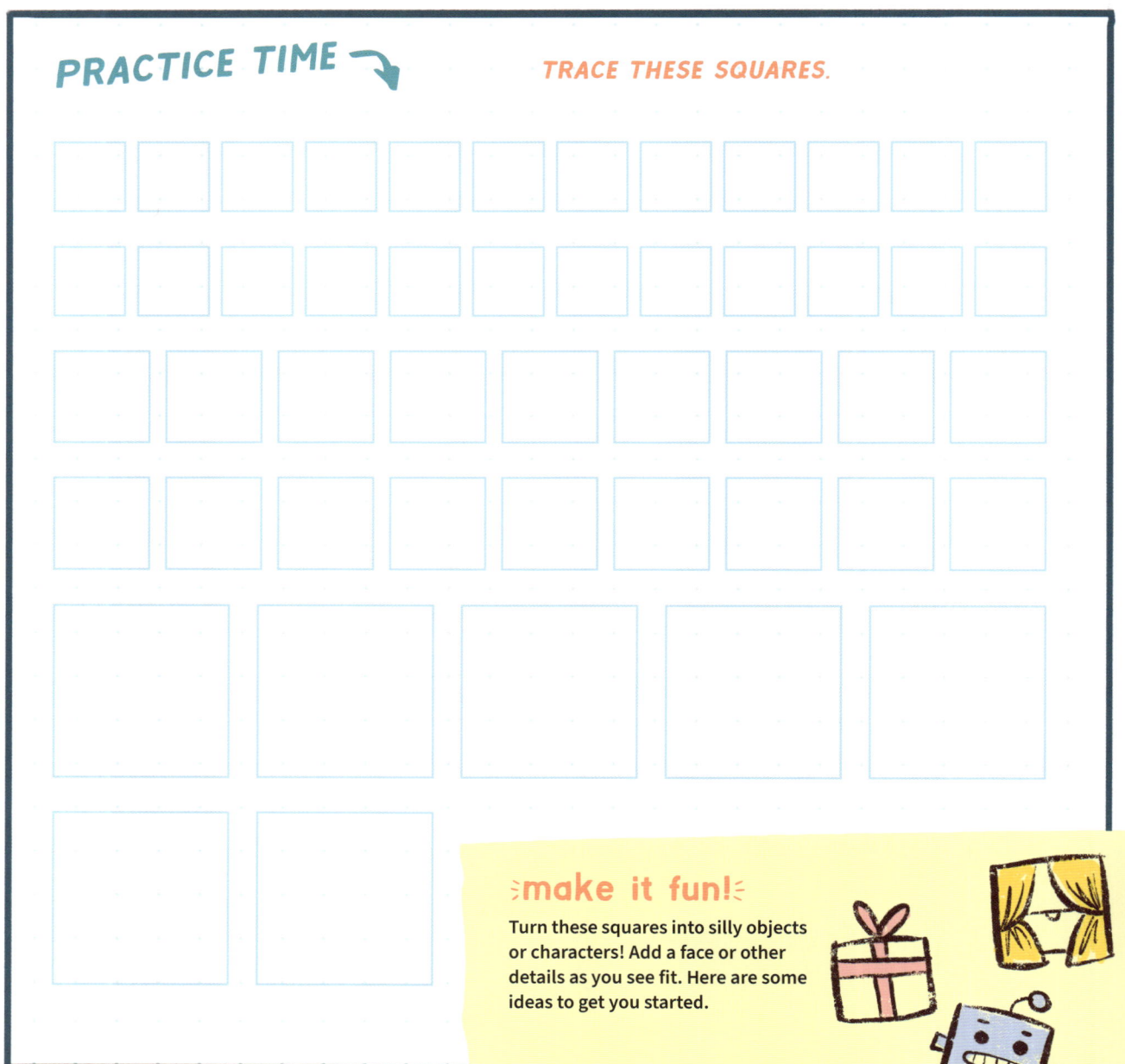

FILL THIS PAGE WITH GIFT BOXES.

ALL OF THIS FOR ME? YOU'RE SO SWEET!

PRACTICE TIME ↘

TRACE THESE TRIANGLES.

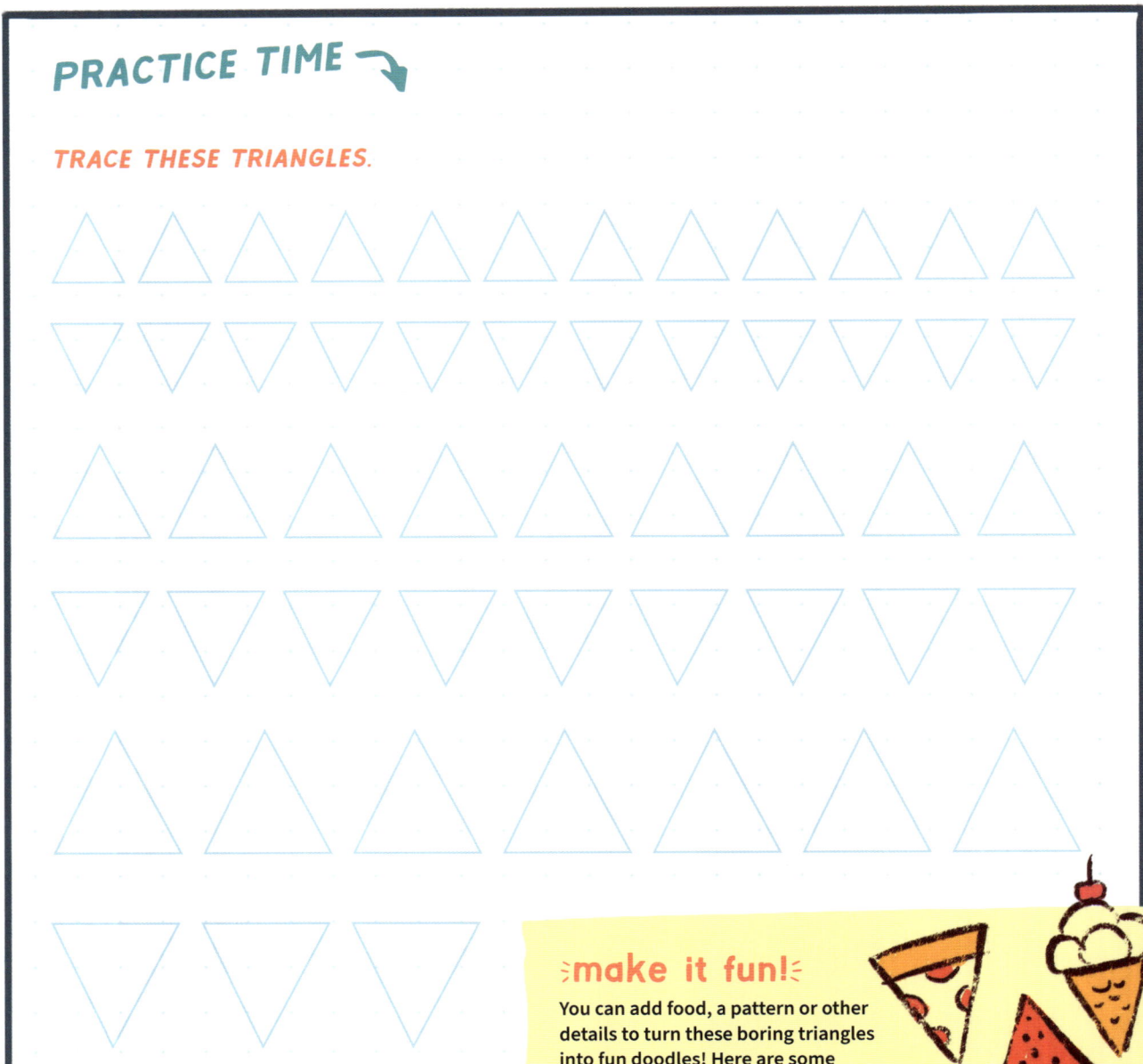

make it fun!
You can add food, a pattern or other details to turn these boring triangles into fun doodles! Here are some ideas to get you started.

SURPRISE, IT'S CONFETTI TIME! FILL THIS PAGE WITH DIFFERENT SIZES OF TRIANGULAR CONFETTI.

SHAPING THINGS UP

PRACTICE TIME

USING DIFFERENT KINDS OF SHAPES, CAN YOU TAKE THIS LITTLE DINO AND MAKE HIM FEEL LIKE . . .

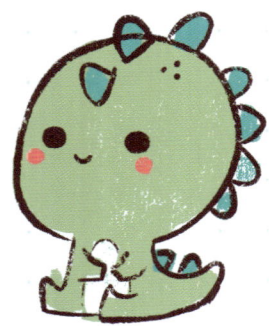

. . . A VERY FRIENDLY DINO?

. . . A BORING DINO?

. . . A DANGEROUS DINO?

USE SIMPLE SHAPES TO FILL THIS PAGE WITH VINES, PLANTS, OR FLOWERS.

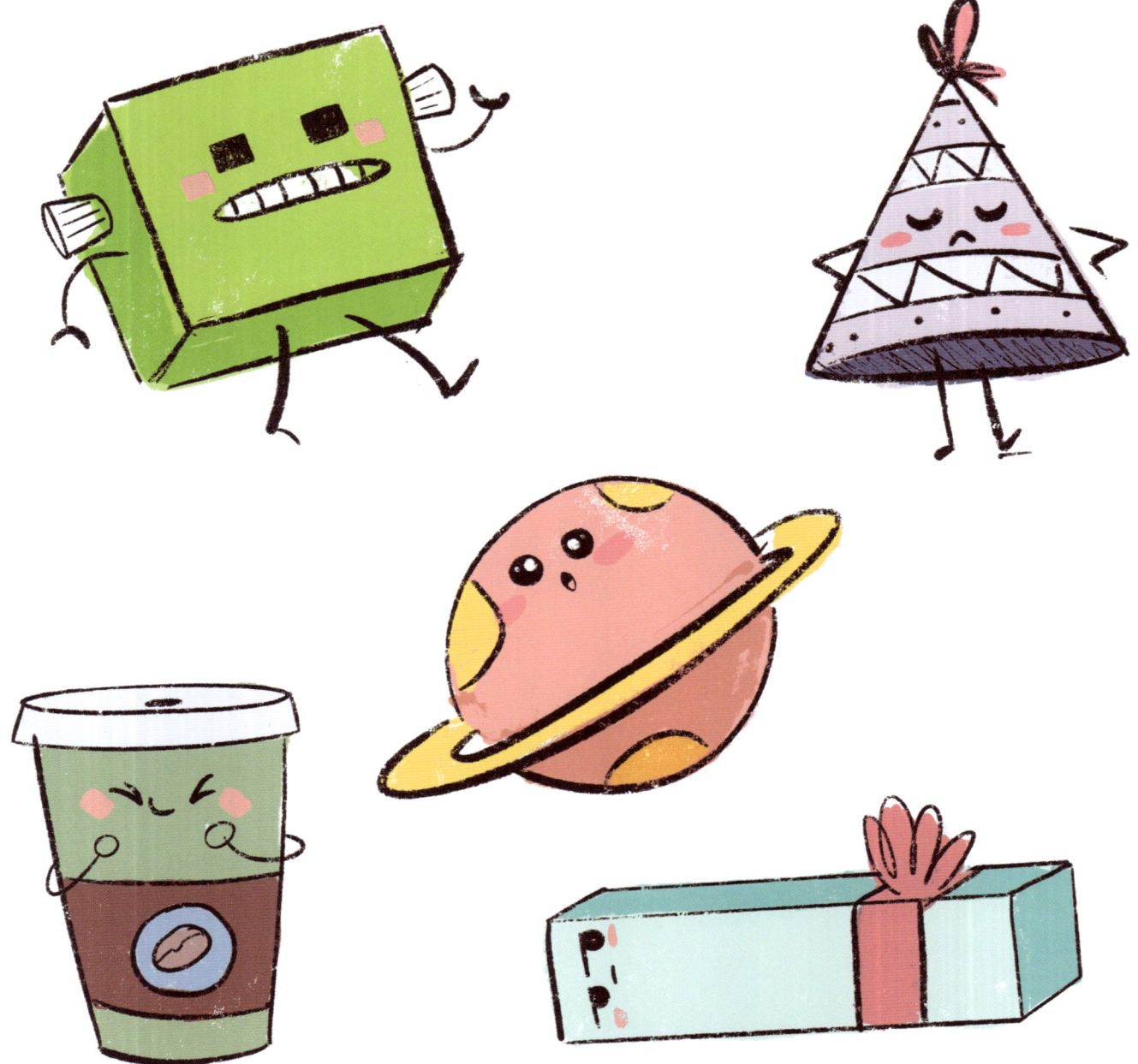

LET'S ADD VOLUME

IT'S TIME FOR THE ART OF ILLUSION! YOU'LL NOW LEARN HOW TO MAKE YOUR DRAWINGS POP OFF THE PAGE!

There's something about making a couple of lines on a flat piece of paper look like they're 3D or have volume that is SO rewarding! I feel like a magician making my little drawings pop off the page and appear to have depth and distance.

When I first learned how to draw cubes, pyramids, and similar shapes, I found it kind of mysterious, but eventually I learned a step-by-step method that made it actually super simple. So here are my secret tips!

Ready to make some magic?

creating volume

When I say we are taking a 2D shape and making it 3D, I'm talkin' a square into a cube, a circle into a sphere, and other shapes like that. I've got some easy tricks up my sleeve to help you!

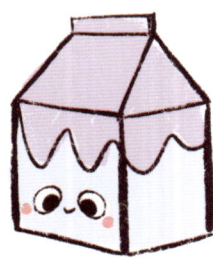

TURN A SQUARE INTO A CUBE

By overlapping two squares and connecting the corners, you can easily make a cube!

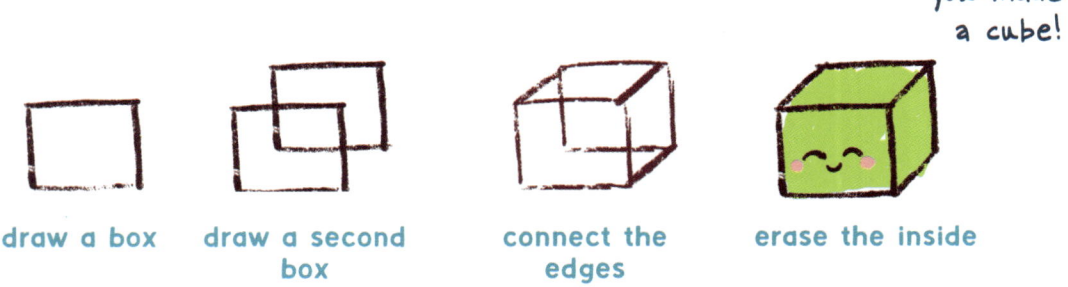

draw a box   draw a second box   connect the edges   erase the inside

you made a cube!

OR A RECTANGLE INTO A CUBOID

I just learned a 3D rectangle is called a cuboid. Look at us, learning together.

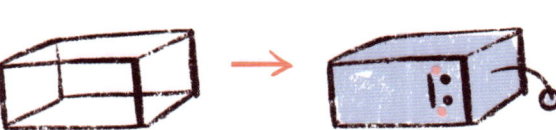

you made a cuboid!

50 THE CUTEST BEGINNER DRAWING BOOK EVER

VARY THIS UP A BIT

Now you can try drawing squares that overlap at different distances. You can also try only erasing part of the box to make it look like it's open!

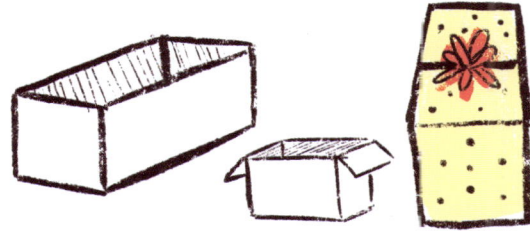
this box is open!

TRY A LITTLE TILT

Next you're going to practice squares at different angles. You can skew the square or tilt them. Can you make it seem like we are looking at the bottom or the top of your square?

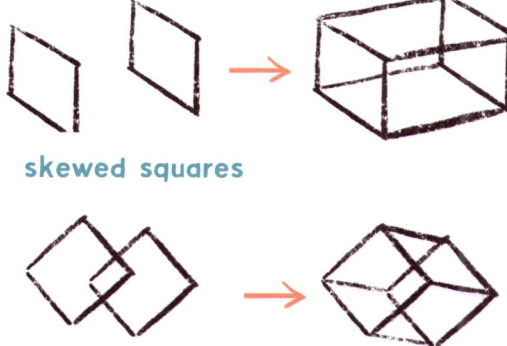
skewed squares

tilted squares

GET READY FOR PERSPECTIVE

If you can make the back square smaller than the front square, then you'll be doing the first step to learn perspective.

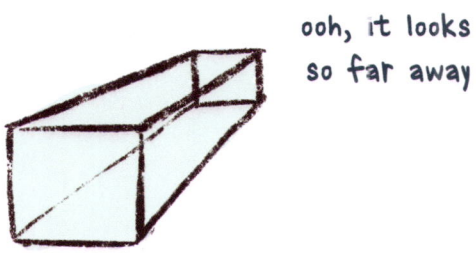
ooh, it looks so far away

LET'S ADD VOLUME 51

cones, pyramids, and tubes

If you apply what you learned with the cubes to other kinds of shapes, they become pretty easy, too!

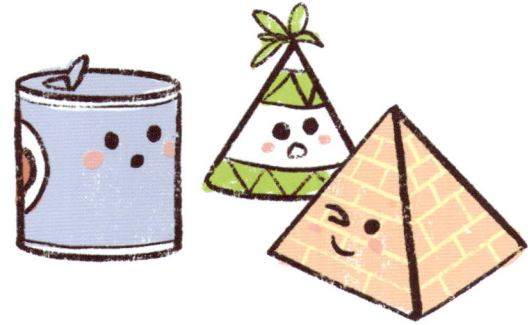

TUBES

Tubes are made the same way you made a cube! You'll just be connecting two ovals or circles together instead of two squares.

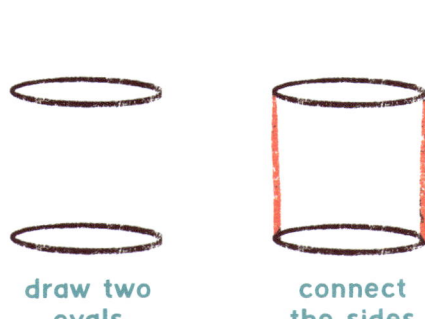

draw two ovals

connect the sides

PYRAMIDS AND CONES

Draw the base (a square or an oval) and then connect the sides to a single point.

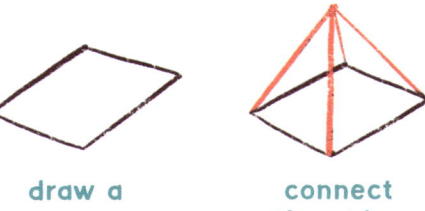

draw a square

connect the sides

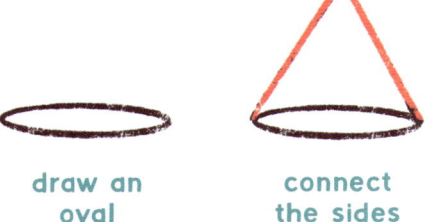

draw an oval

connect the sides

spheres and round objects

Round shapes can be a bit more tricky, but you can add just a little bit of form with these sneaky tips.

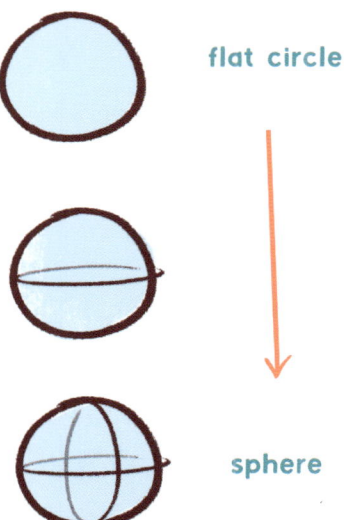

flat circle

sphere

SILLY SPHERES

Spheres are kind of funny because without any markings, they look like a circle. So just add some markings like a seam or a highlight!

ROUNDISH SHAPES, TOO

You can add ovals to objects that should be round to make them feel less flat, too! This is especially helpful when drawing people.

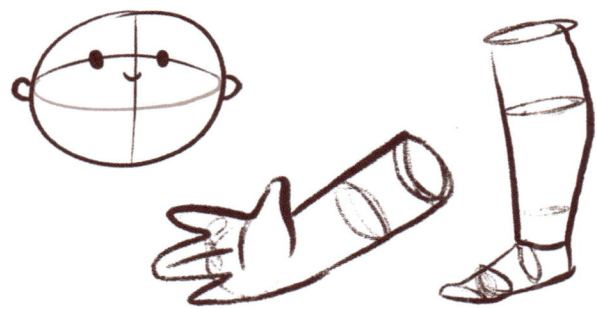

LET'S ADD VOLUME 53

draw anything simply . . . again!

Now that you know how to draw shapes with volume, you can use these shapes to simplify more complex things.

FLAT SHAPES THEN ROUND SHAPES

Even when drawing in a more detailed style, you can start with simple shapes to create your sketch and then add details after.

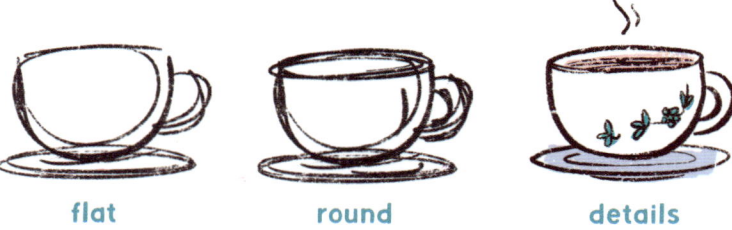

flat — round — details

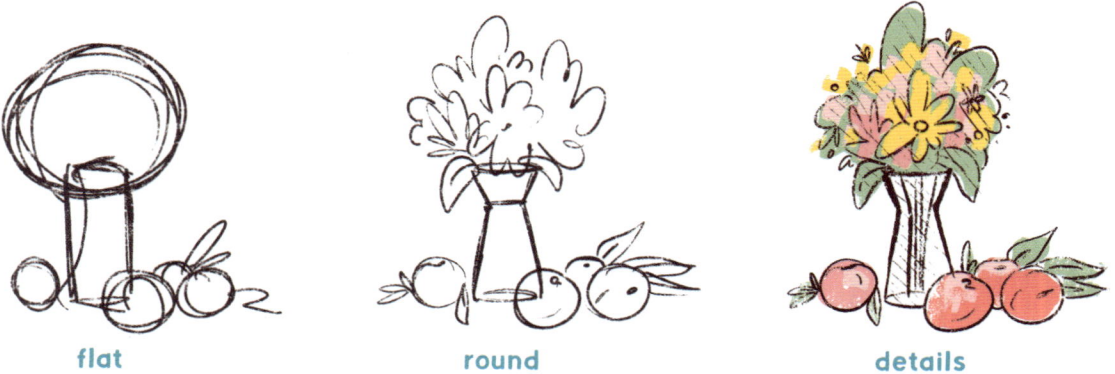

flat — round — details

54 THE CUTEST BEGINNER DRAWING BOOK EVER

what about style?

Choosing to draw things with volume is a style choice! Here's the difference between flat drawing styles and volumetric drawing styles. Which one do you prefer?

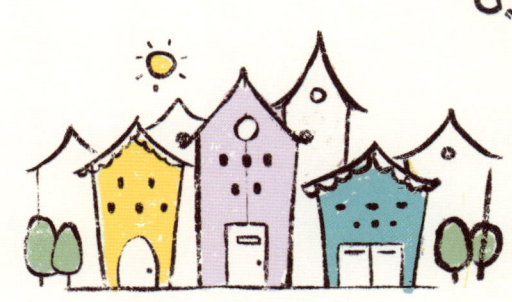

FLAT DRAWING STYLE

In this style you'll keep to simple shapes and won't add volume or depth. It's a very simplistic style, great for kids' books!

flat and simple

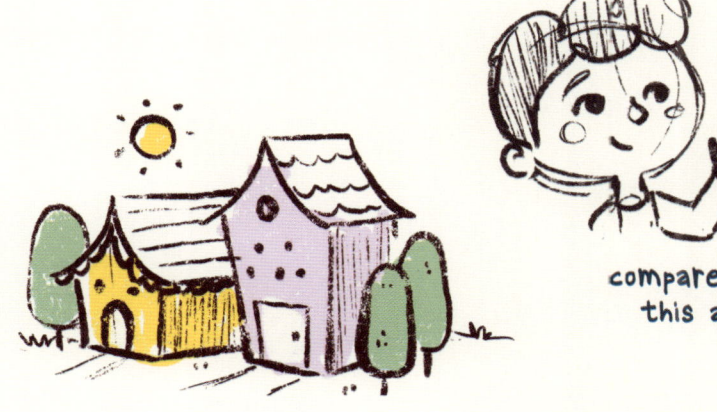

VOLUMETRIC DRAWING STYLE

When you use volume, you're drawing in a way that's more true to life. You don't have to draw perfectly realistic, but there is volume and depth.

has depth

LET'S ADD VOLUME

PRACTICE TIME

TURN SOME SQUARES OR RECTANGLES INTO CUBES OR CUBOIDS.

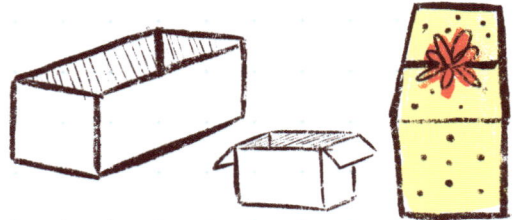

make it fun!
You can add a face, a pattern or other details to turn these boring cubes into fun doodles! Here's some ideas to get you started.

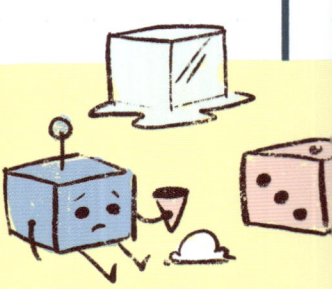

NOW TILT OR SKEW YOUR SQUARES OR RECTANGLES BEFORE BUILDING YOUR CUBE.

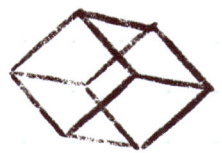

TRY A FEW WITH SMALLER BOXES IN THE BACK.

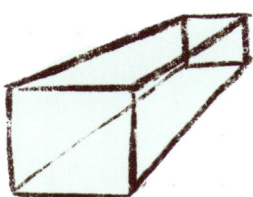

LET'S ADD VOLUME 57

PRACTICE TIME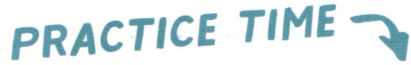

DRAW THE GREAT PYRAMIDS OF EGYPT OR SOME CAMPING TENTS.

DRAW SOME ICE CREAM CONES AND PARTY HATS!

DRAW A CAN OF SODA, A COFFEE CUP, OR SOMETHING ELSE TOTALLY TUBULAR.

DRAW SOME BUBBLES, BOUNCY BALLS, OR ROUND FRUIT.

LET'S ADD VOLUME 59

PRACTICE TIME ↘

YOUR TURN! DRAW THESE OBJECTS STARTING WITH SIMPLE SHAPES FIRST.

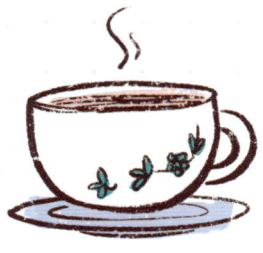

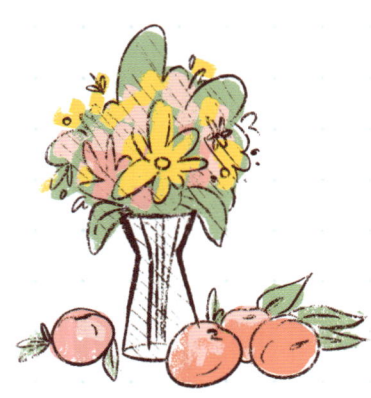

DRAW THIS WITH A FLAT DRAWING STYLE.

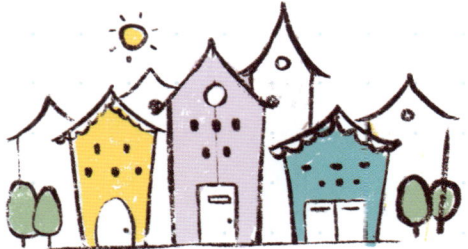

DRAW IT AGAIN WITH A VOLUMETRIC DRAWING STYLE.

WHICH STYLE DO YOU LIKE BETTER?

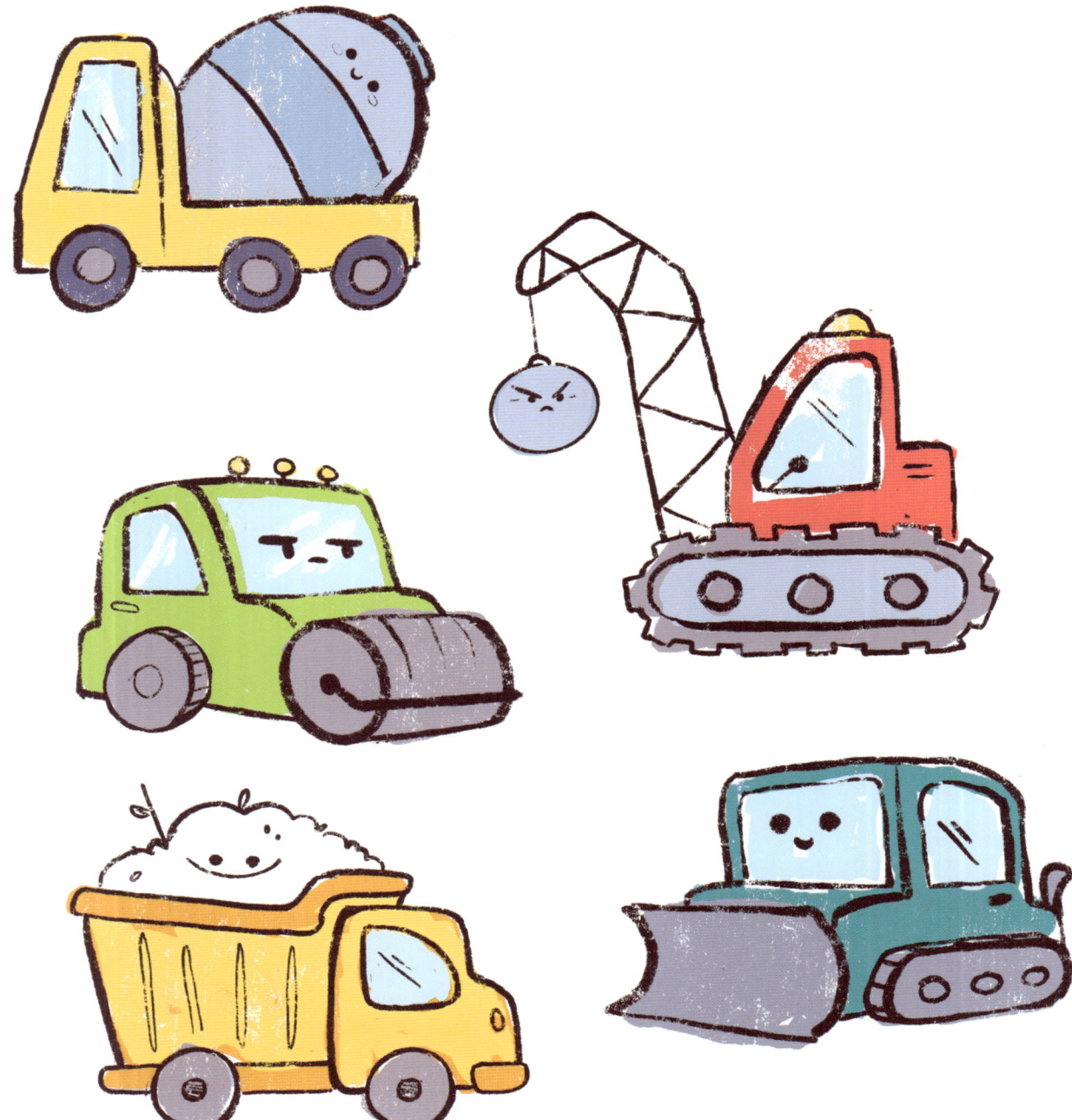

CONSTRUCTING NEW SHAPES

NOW IT'S TIME TO COMBINE THE SHAPES YOU'VE LEARNED SO FAR TO DRAW JUST ABOUT ANYTHING!

You now have the building blocks to create all the things you want. In this chapter I'll show you how to use simple shapes and round shapes combined to draw more complex things!

You'll take the circles and cubes that you've learned to draw and either carve out new shapes or combine them to make something new.

Yay, let's build some cute drawings!

creating new shapes

We can also use our basic shapes as a starting point and cut new shapes out of them. Like this!

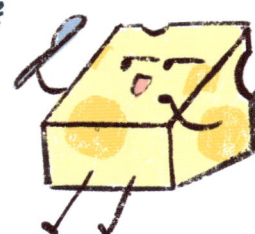

GRAB A SLICE

By slicing into our first object, we can create new shapes.

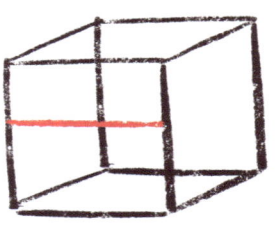
draw an inner line

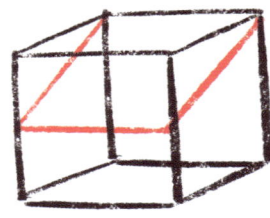
connect to the corners

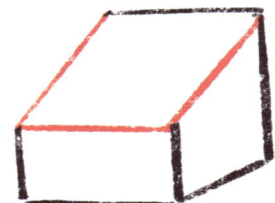
erase the top

CARVE SHAPES OUT

As long as you keep the new lines you draw parallel, you can cut out all kinds of shapes!

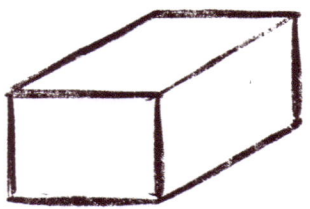
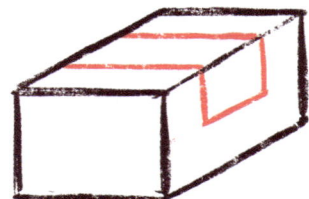
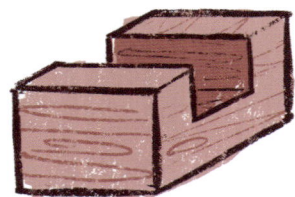

FIND AN INNER OVAL

I can also add an oval shape inside of another object and erase what I don't want.

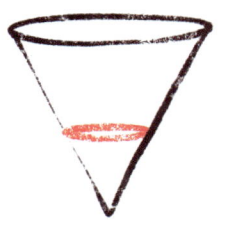 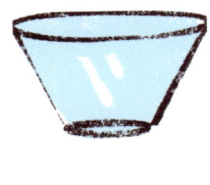

cut off the bottom

 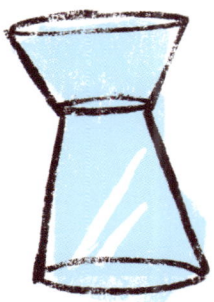

squeeze in the middle

CREATE A SEMICIRCLE

You can also use cubes to make semicircles or tunnels like this.

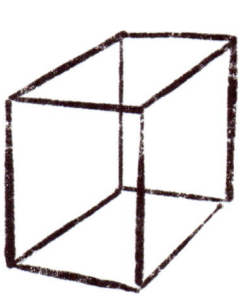 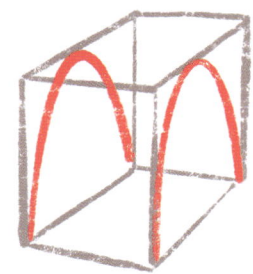 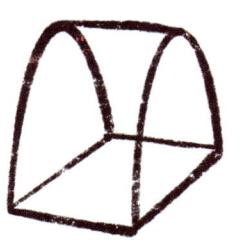

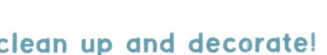

start with a box

draw your round shapes inside the box edges

clean up and decorate!

use your building blocks

We are now going to use all the basic shapes we've learned to create more complex things! In art this is called construction. You're building your drawing piece by piece.

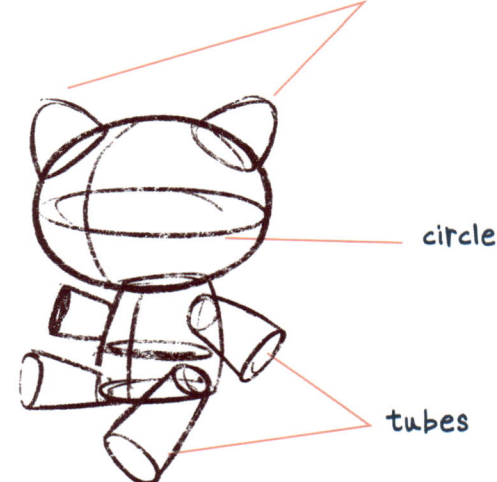

USE YOUR SIMPLE SHAPES

First I'll take all the parts of the object and choose some simple shapes that are similar to them.

DRAW OVER AND CLEAN

After you have your basic shapes, you can either trace, or draw darker over top, to decide on the outline shapes.

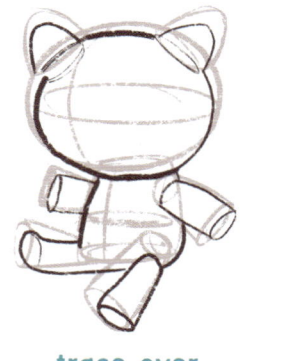

trace over

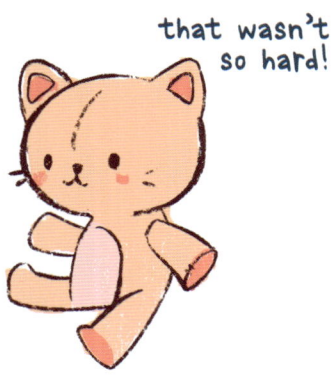

add details

that wasn't so hard!

ROUND SHARP EDGES AS NEEDED

I sometimes will use square shapes first and then round the edges at the end. It's also extra cute that way!

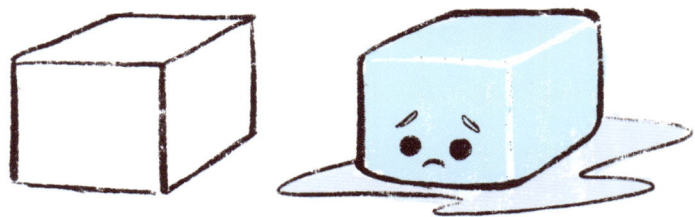

NOW YOU'RE MAKIN' COMPLEX STUFF!

Combine the tips above and you'll be able to break down complicated objects with ease.

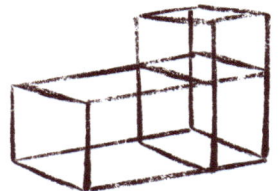 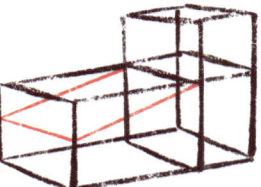

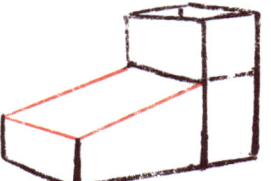 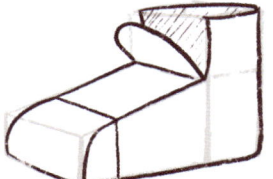 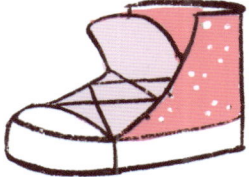

PRACTICE TIME ↘

DEEP BREATH, YOU'VE GOT THIS! DRAW THESE COMPLEX THINGS.

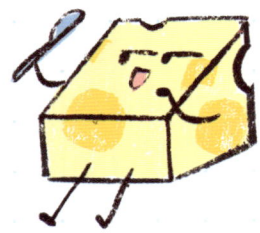

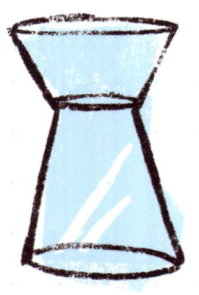

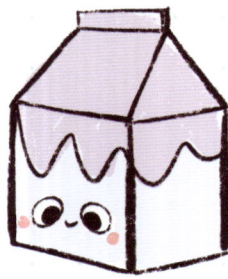

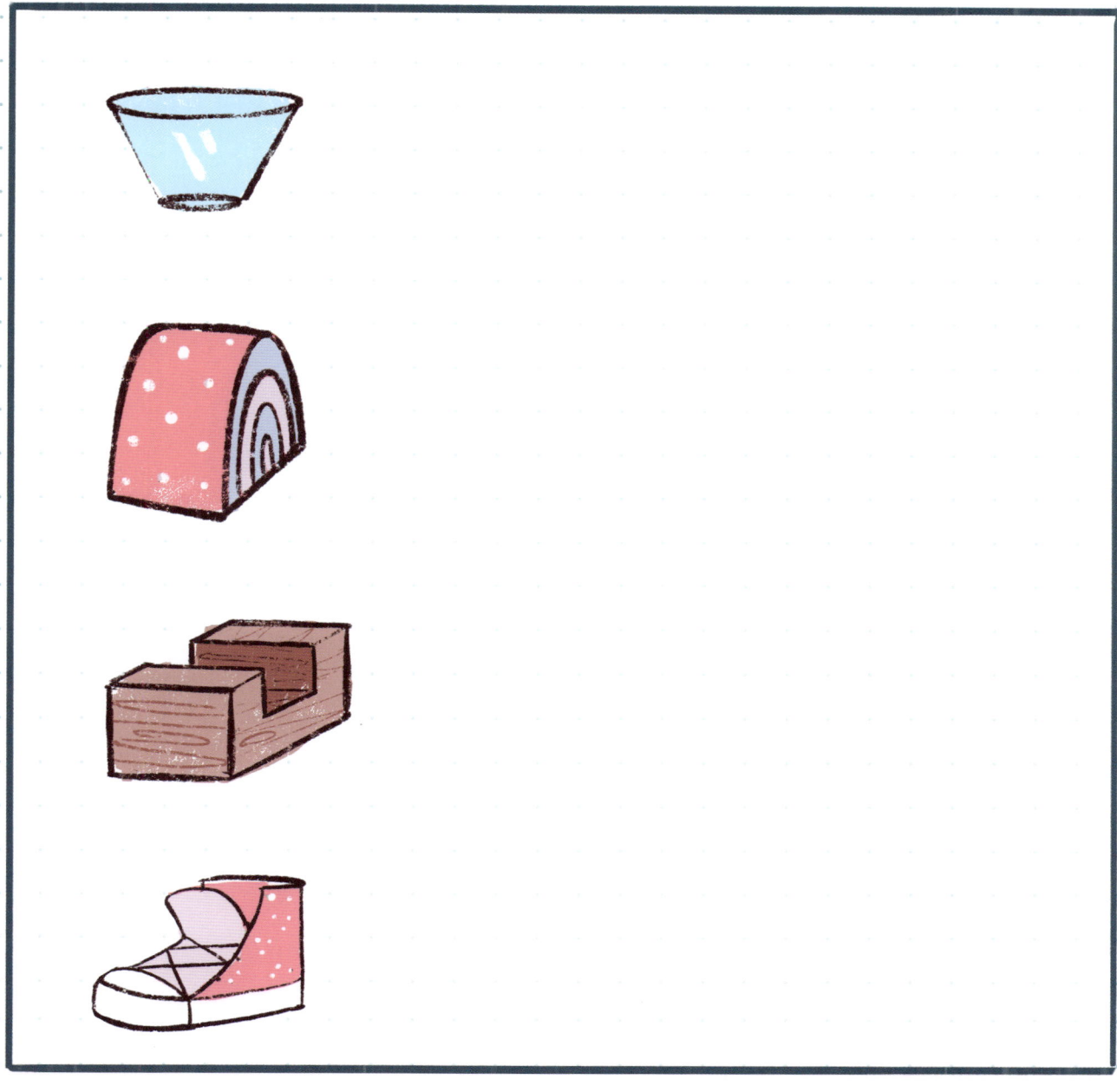

CONSTRUCTING NEW SHAPES **69**

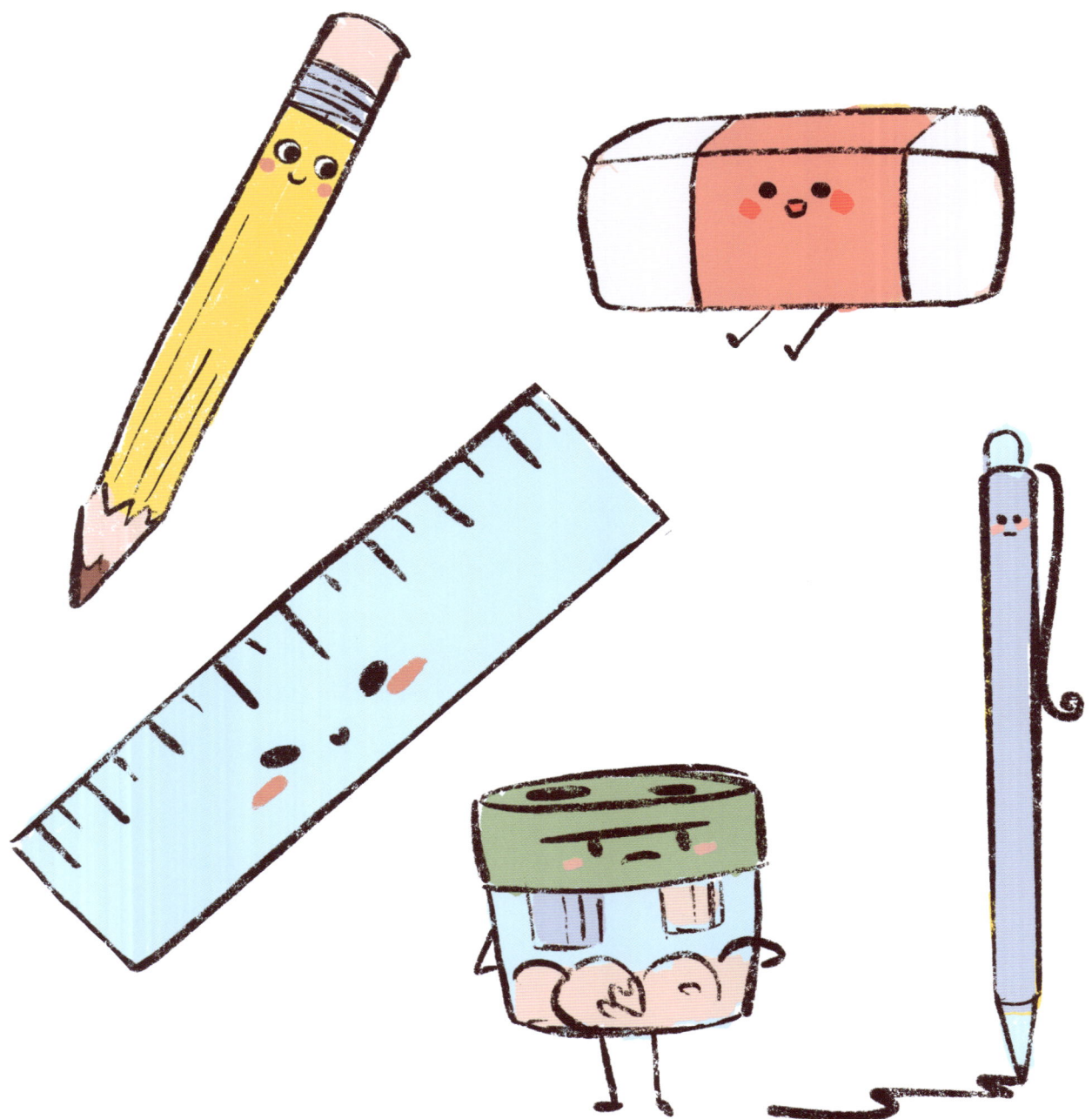

JUST A LIL' PERSPECTIVE

PUT YOUR RULER DOWN. THAT'S NOT WHAT WE'RE DOING HERE.

I'm going to be honest, perspective was SO scary to me as a beginner artist! One look at those complex grids to show how to draw a city and I was immediately overwhelmed. So I am going to have a simpler approach to perspective. It's super important you read the earlier chapter, because you'll need those skills for this one.

I'll explain a few types of perspective (there are more than you might think). I'll try to teach you the most important tips and as always keep it fun.

Ready? Let's get some perspective!

what even is perspective?

Perspective is all the little tricks artists use to make what is actually a flat drawing look like it has depth. It's the art of illusion!

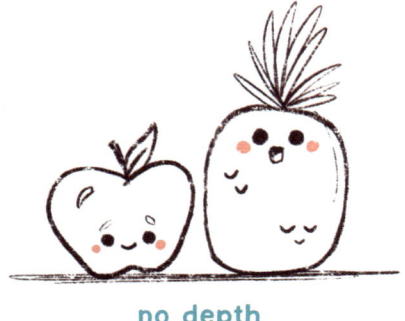

no depth

ALL ABOUT CREATING DEPTH

Depth means that some things look closer to us than other things. Here's some ways to create depth using different kinds of perspective tricks.

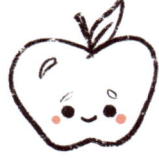 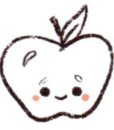 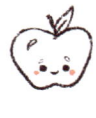

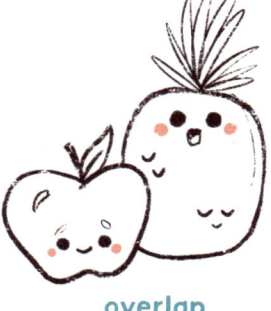

overlap

change in value

change in color

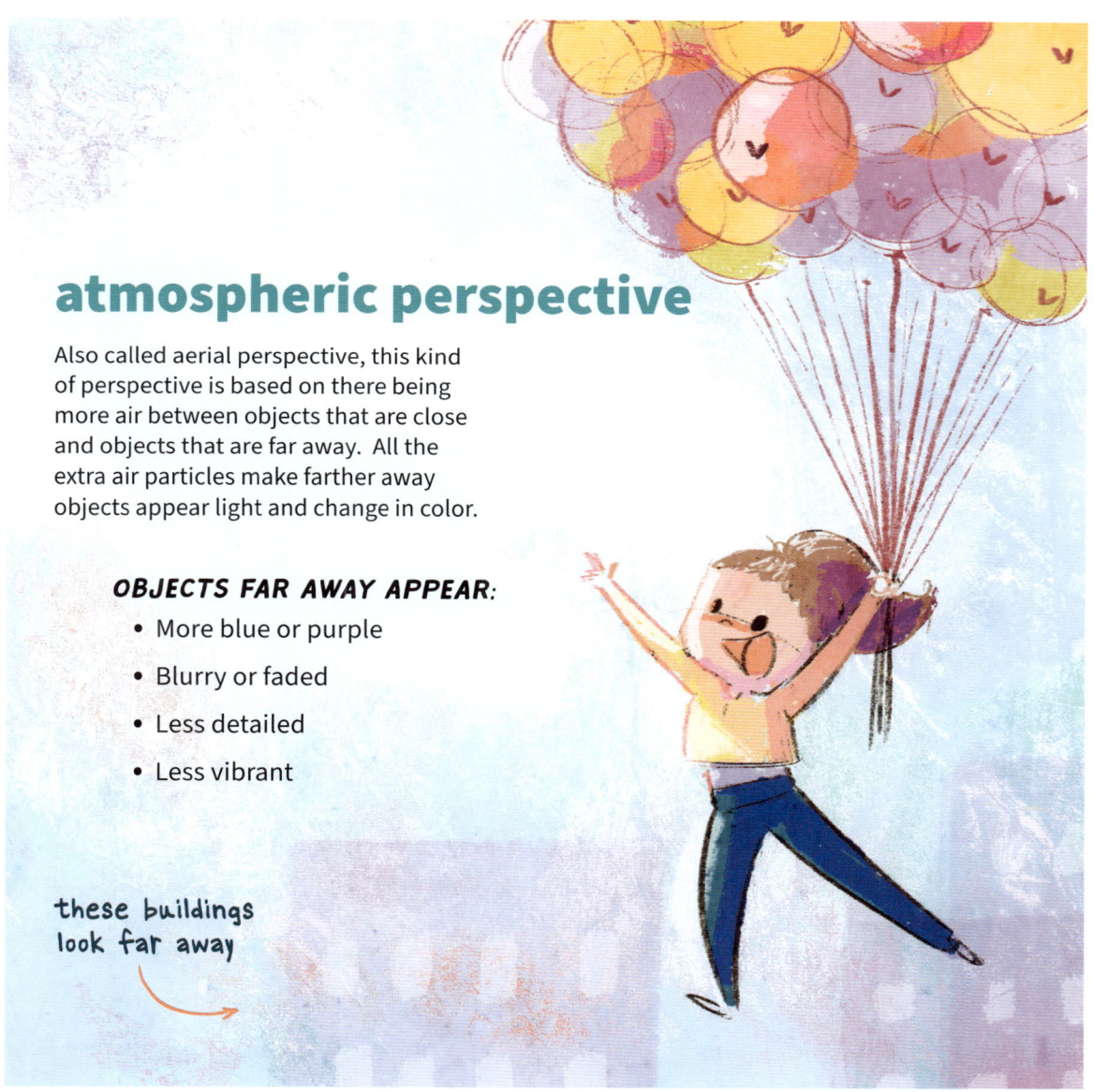

atmospheric perspective

Also called aerial perspective, this kind of perspective is based on there being more air between objects that are close and objects that are far away. All the extra air particles make farther away objects appear light and change in color.

OBJECTS FAR AWAY APPEAR:
- More blue or purple
- Blurry or faded
- Less detailed
- Less vibrant

these buildings look far away

JUST A LIL' PERSPECTIVE

linear perspective

The perspective you're probably most familiar with is called "linear perspective." It's all about how the lines in your drawing are used to create depth.

HORIZON LINE

When drawing with this kind of perspective, the first step is to find your horizon line. This is where the sky meets with the surface of the earth.

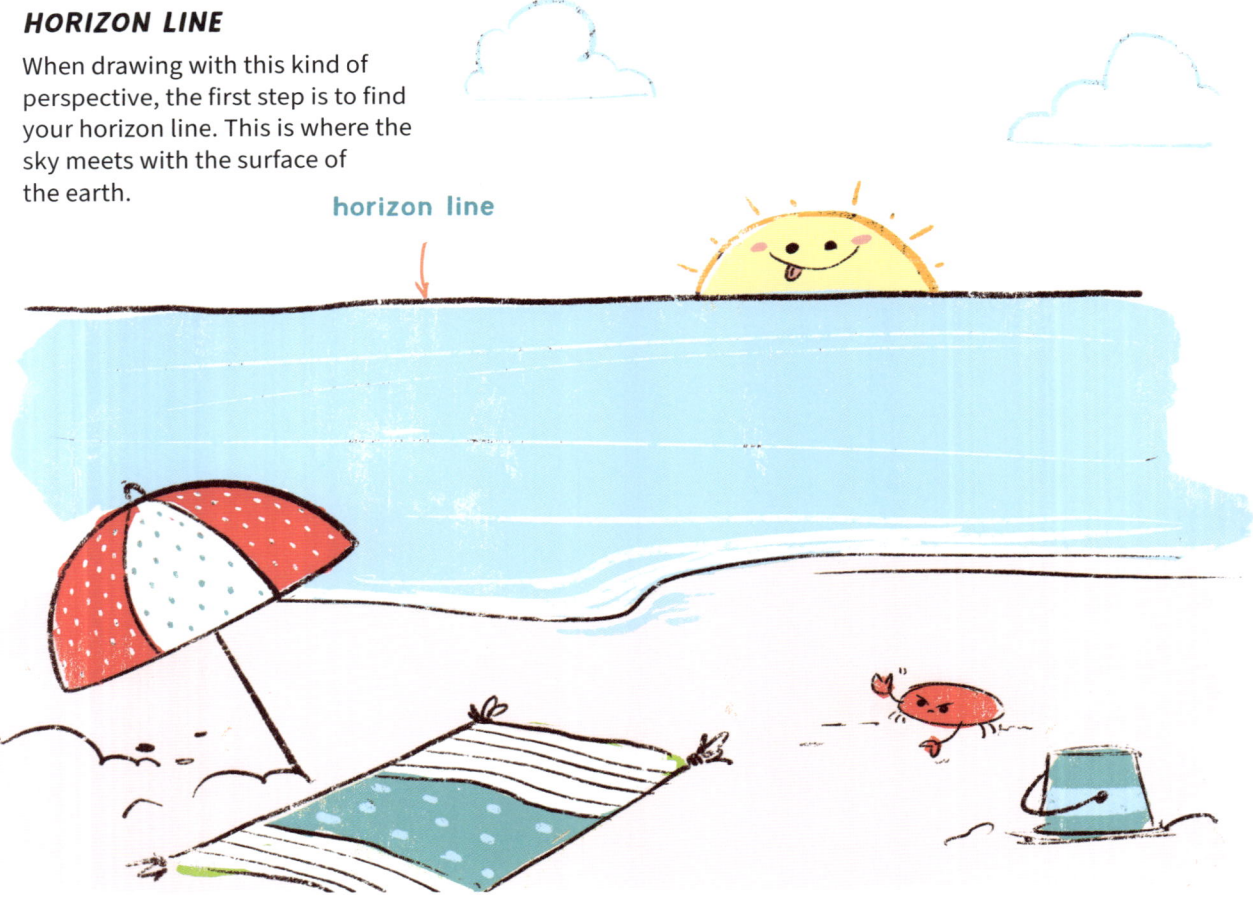

horizon line

EYE LEVEL

When you look around the world, the horizon is at eye level. So you can often use a character's eye line to find the horizon line.

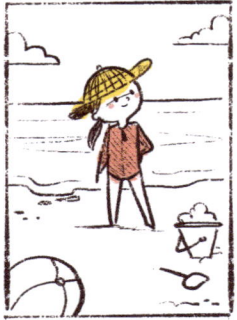
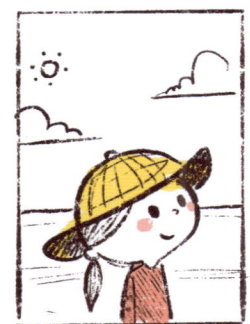

PLACING CHARACTERS IN THE DISTANCE

Characters that are the same height will have their eyes on the horizon line. Then you can use a line to place their feet on the ground. Here's how I would draw two adults and a kid in a scene.

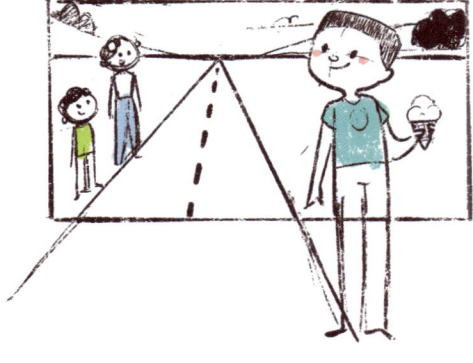

CAMERA LEVEL CHANGES

In extreme views the horizon line is below or above the character's eye line. This is because the "camera angle," or where we are looking at the image from changes to be low or high.

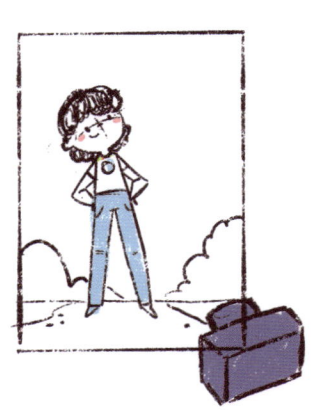
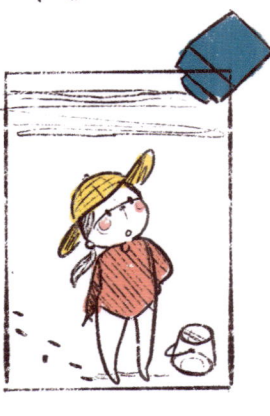

JUST A LIL' PERSPECTIVE

a disappearing act

In linear perspective, everything disappears to the same point, called a vanishing point. So first you need to find out where that is.

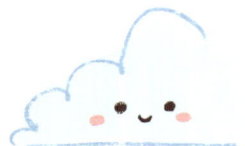

THE VANISHING POINT

When drawing the different kinds of perspective, lines will disappear to one or more vanishing points, like this road and the trees.

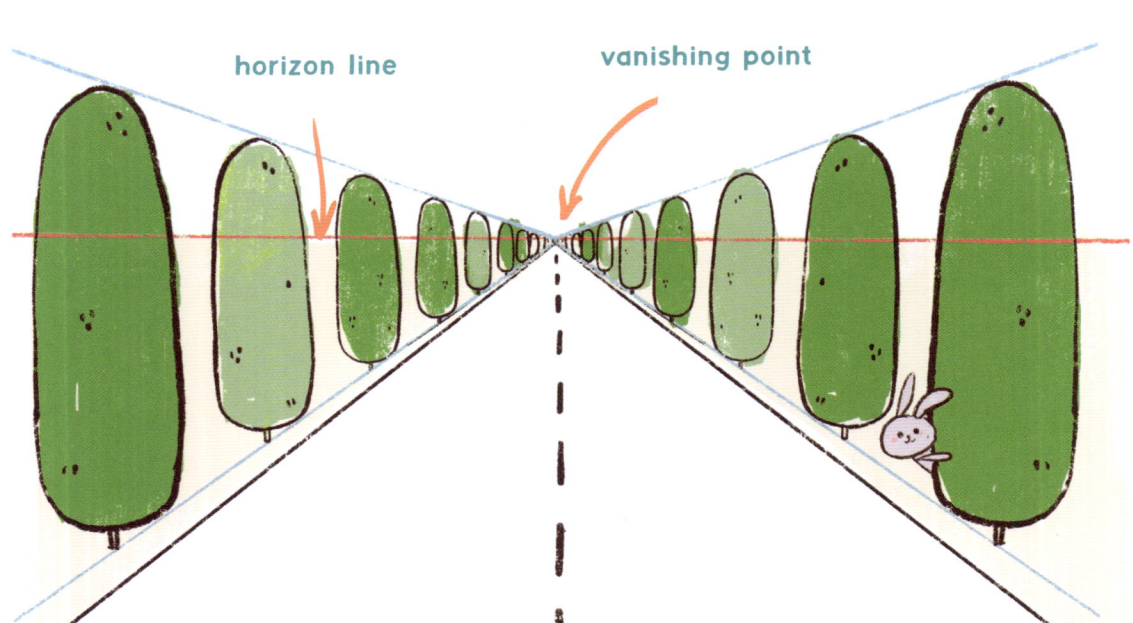

horizon line   vanishing point

VANISHING OFF SCREEN

The vanishing point you use might not be in the picture, but off to the side somewhere. The farther away the vanishing point is from your image, the less extreme the perspective will seem.

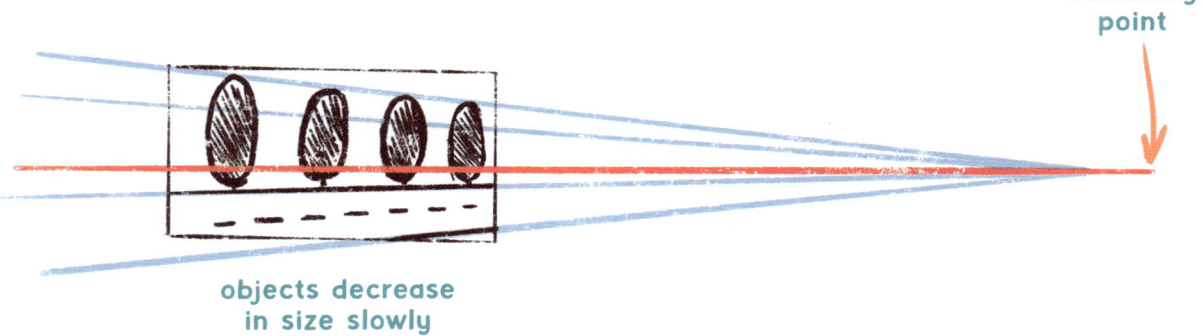

objects decrease in size slowly

NO VANISHING POINT?

When I first taught you how to make shapes, we made them so that each side had lines that were parallel. This is actually called isometric perspective! It's really common in video games or maps where you need to see all the details.

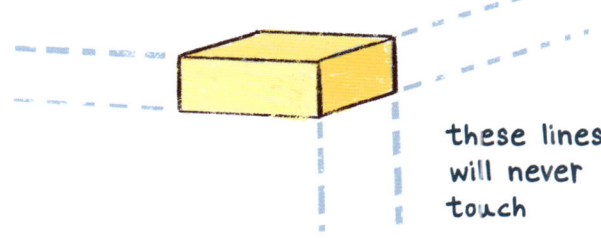

these lines will never touch

JUST A LIL' PERSPECTIVE

three types of perspective

There are three main kinds of perspective and they all depend on the amount of vanishing points in your illustration.

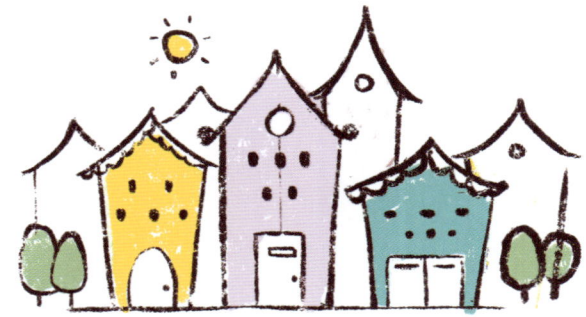

ONE-POINT PERSPECTIVE

This is called one-point perspective because there is only one vanishing point.

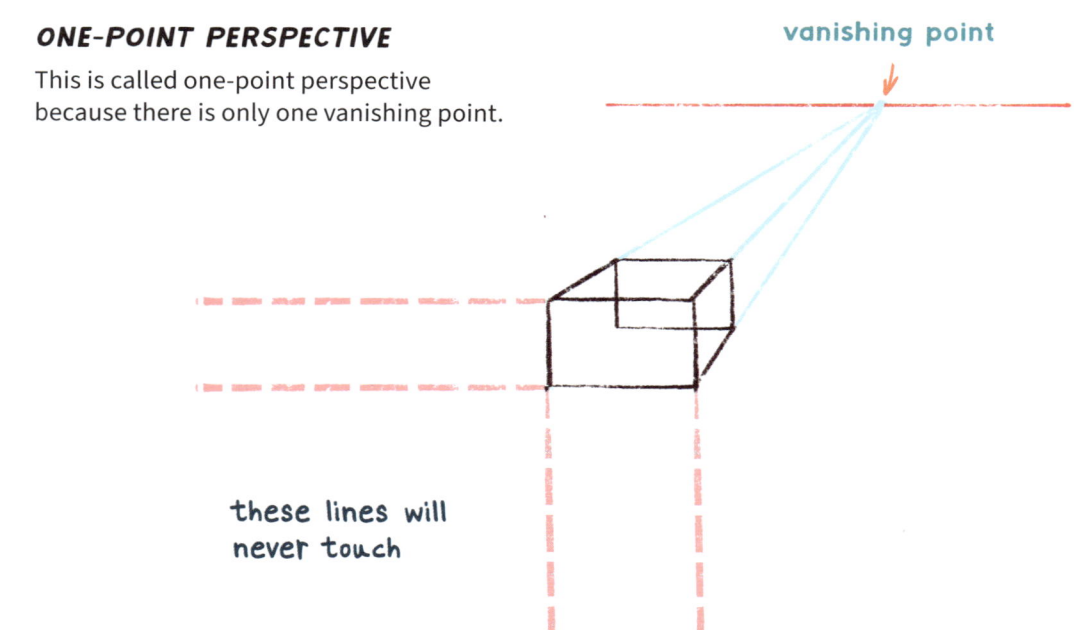

vanishing point

these lines will never touch

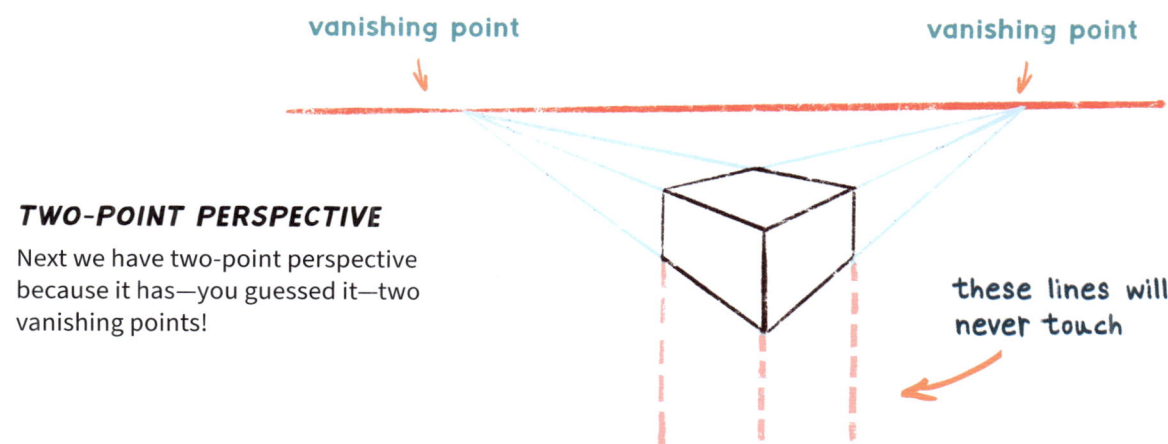

TWO-POINT PERSPECTIVE

Next we have two-point perspective because it has—you guessed it—two vanishing points!

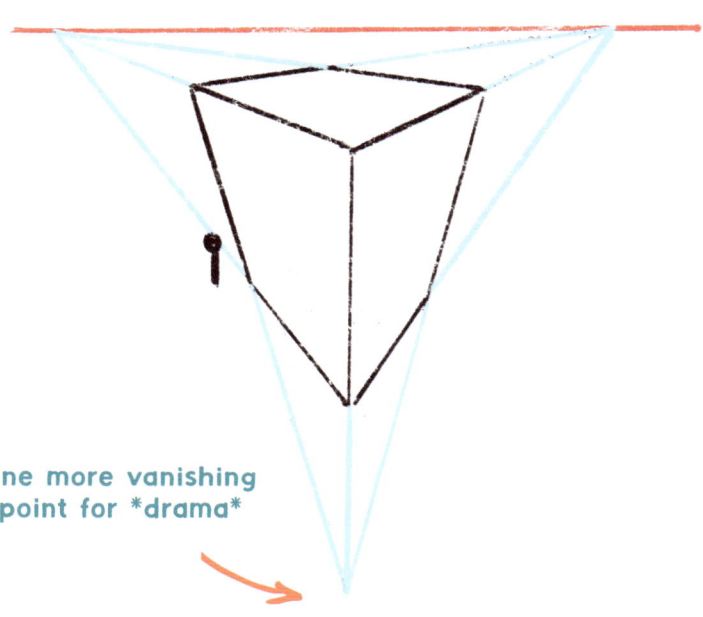

THREE-POINT PERSPECTIVE

Finally, you have three-point perspective. This has two vanishing points on the horizon, and a third one somewhere above or below the horizon line.

JUST A LIL' PERSPECTIVE

how to do it

Here's how I would go about drawing a scene in one-point perspective.

GET SET UP

First you'll need a horizon line and a vanishing point. The blue lines of your grid here can be anywhere so long as they all connect at the vanishing point.

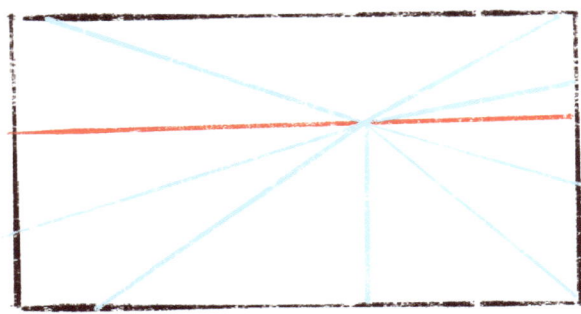

USING THE GRID

Using one line below the horizon and one line above, I can decide where my trees will go on the ground and know how tall they will be.

SIZE AND DISTANCE DECREASE

As objects get farther away, they get smaller and also closer together. The lines in the road and the trees are a good example of this.

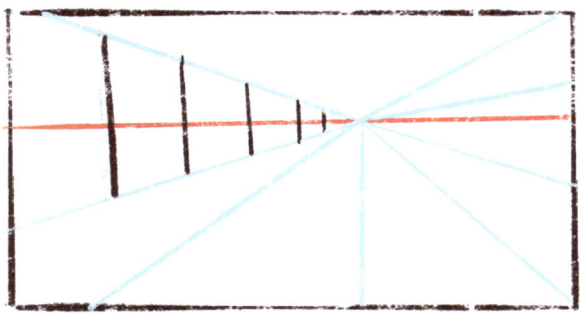

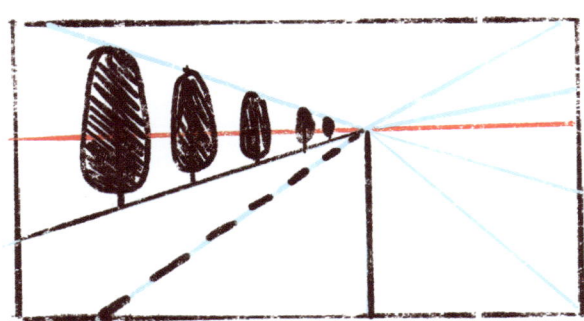

FOR A BUILDING

I can start by drawing the vertical and horizontal lines of my building first. In one-point perspective these lines don't vanish to a point.

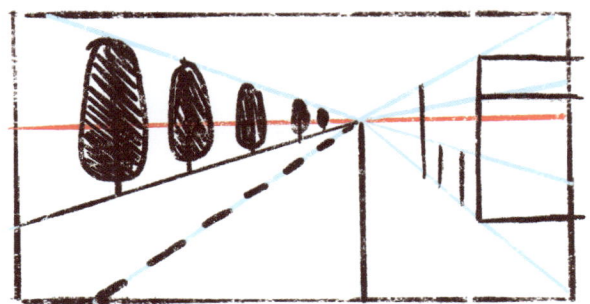

CONNECTING THE SIDES

Then I'll use my grid to draw the lines that connect to the vanishing point.

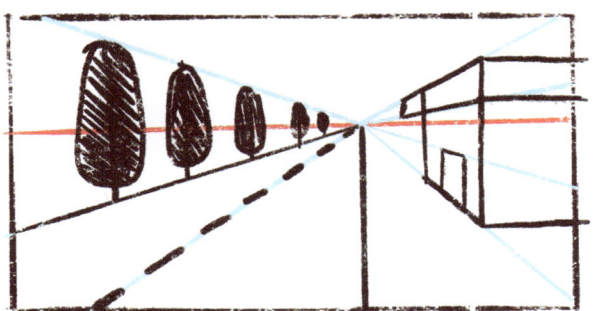

KEEP ON ADDING

I can continue to add more things to the scene so long as they all align with my grid. Or I can add more blue lines if needed.

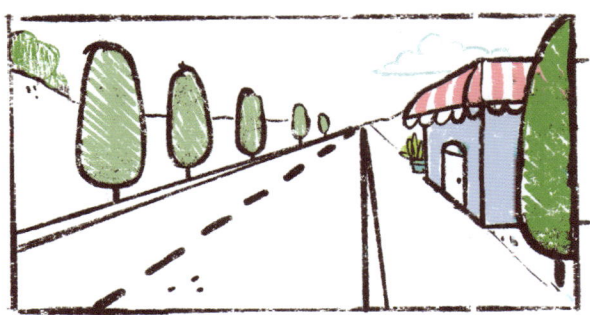

JUST A LIL' PERSPECTIVE

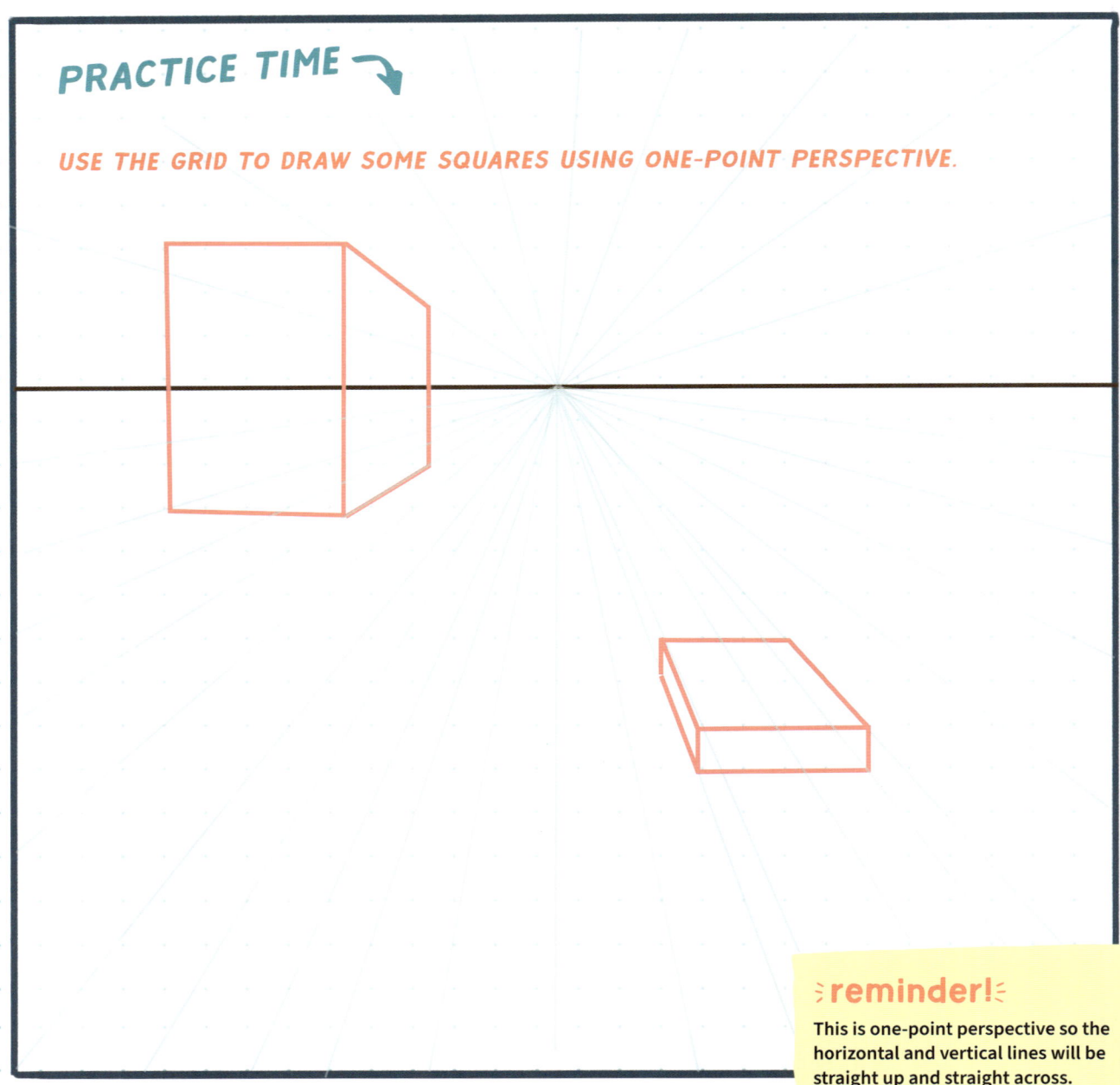

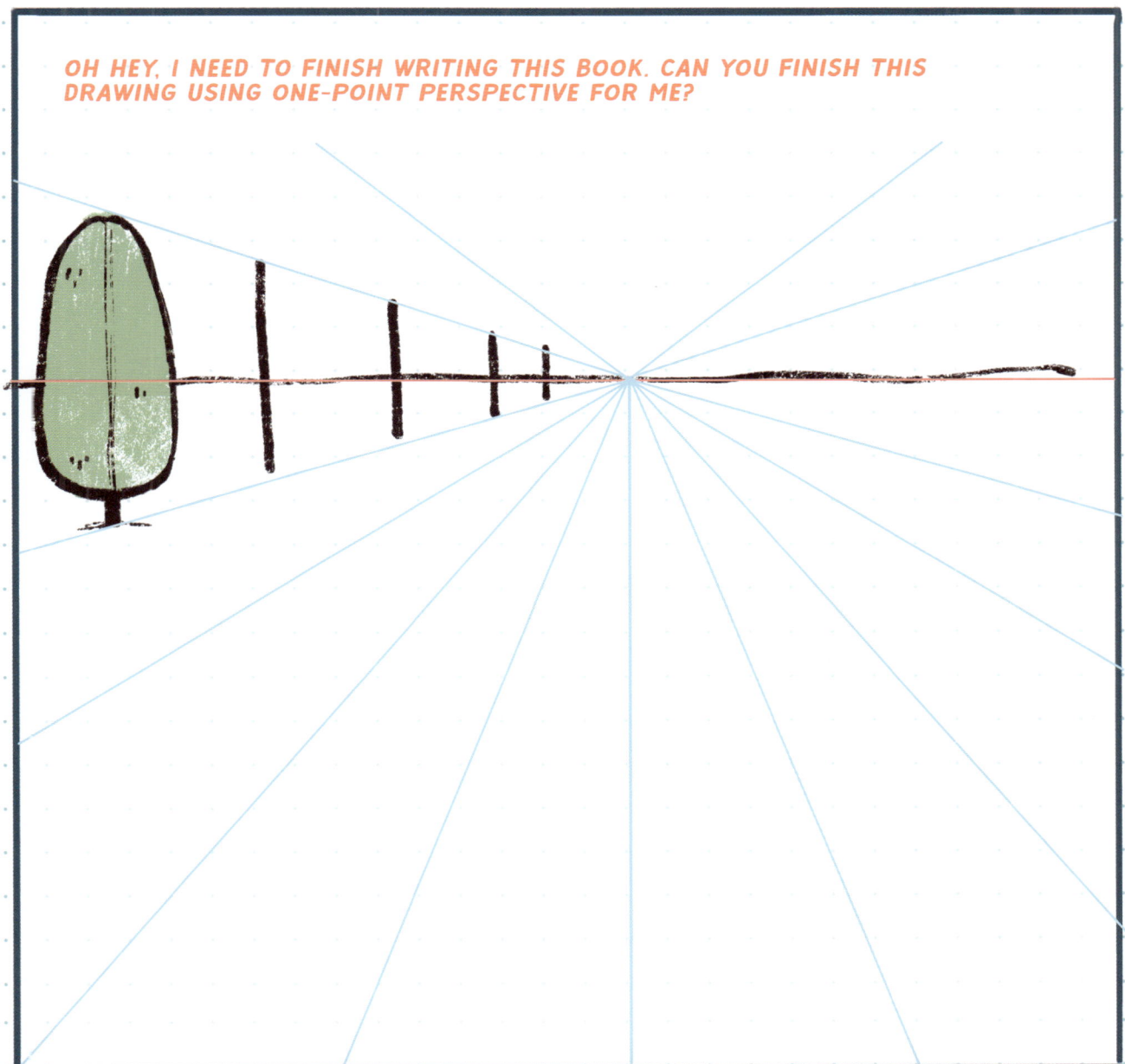

two-points step by step

Here's how I would go about drawing a scene in two-point perspective.

GET SET UP

You can draw a grid here, but to keep life simple, let's just draw a horizon line with two vanishing points on it. Then draw the corner of your object or building.

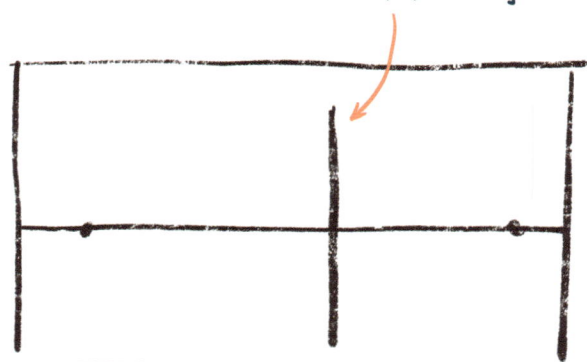

this will be the corner of our building

CONNECT TO THE VANISHING POINT

Now you'll use your vanishing points to draw in a line that connects to what you've drawn already.

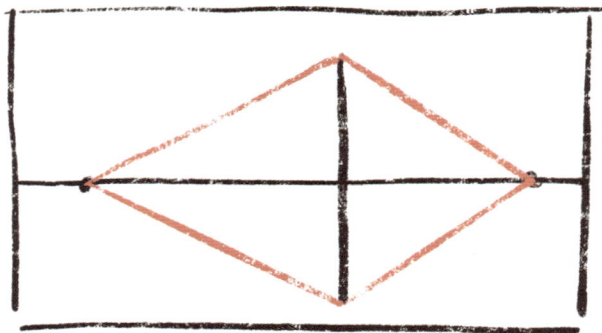

KEEP USING YOUR VANISHING POINTS

Continue to use the vanishing points as your guide to add to your scene. Here I'll add some doors.

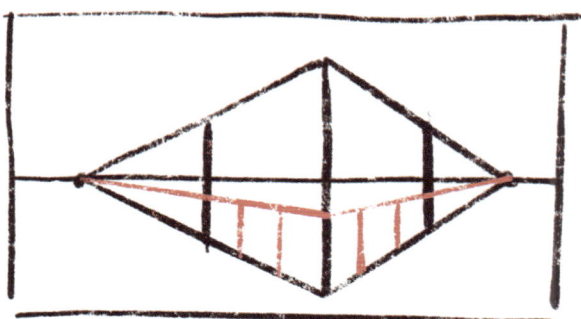

HERE'S HOW OTHER THINGS MIGHT ALIGN

The roads here are both flat, so they can each go to one vanishing point.

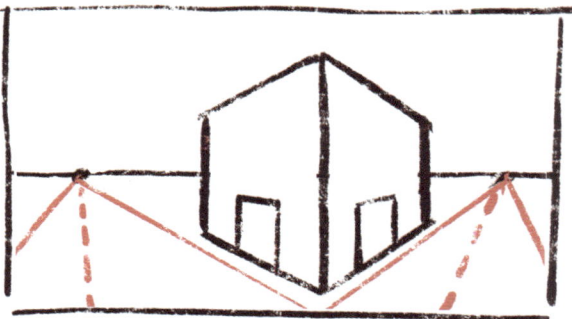

CONTINUE ADDING

Continue this process to complete your illustration.

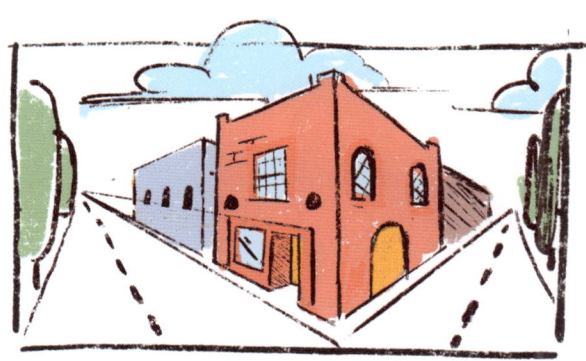

just the basics of three-point perspective

Perfect three-point perspective is truly beyond the scope of a beginner drawing book because it's often only used for super extreme city views. However, you can use the idea of three-point perspective with simple drawings if you just know this one tip.

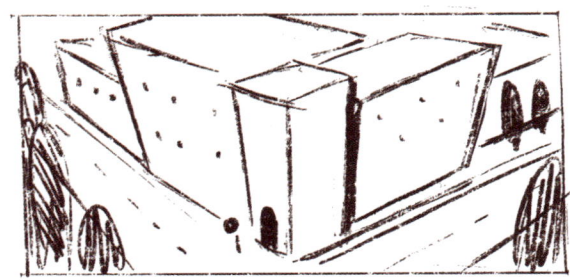

THREE-POINT PERSPECTIVE ADDS DRAMA

The idea is that if you use three-point perspective, you can make something seem dramatically large or small.

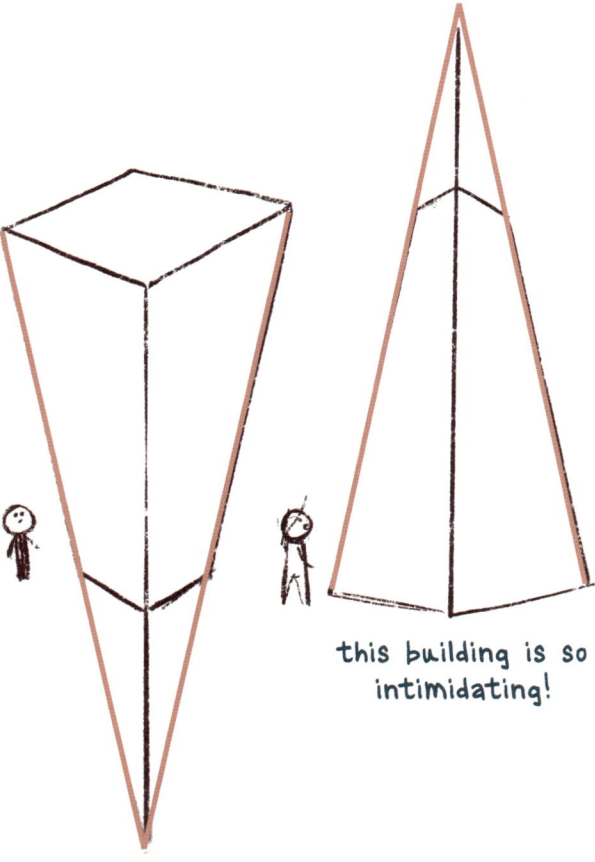

he feels so small!

this building is so intimidating!

CLOSER TO THE CAMERA

The closer something is to a camera, the larger it appears. This is your basic lesson on foreshortening (extreme perspective on a character) and why your nose looks bigger in selfies.

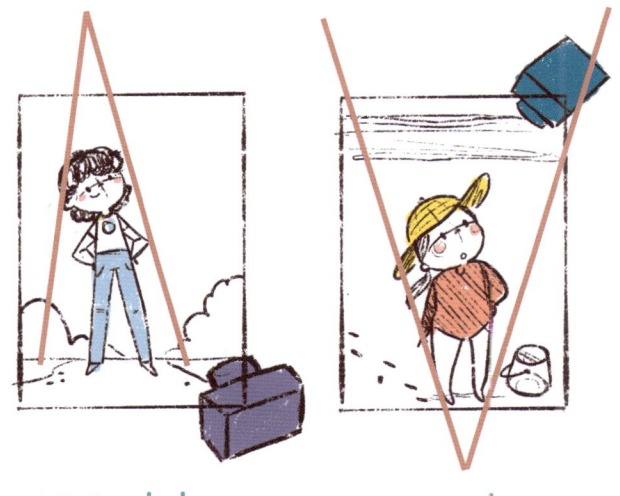

camera below   camera above

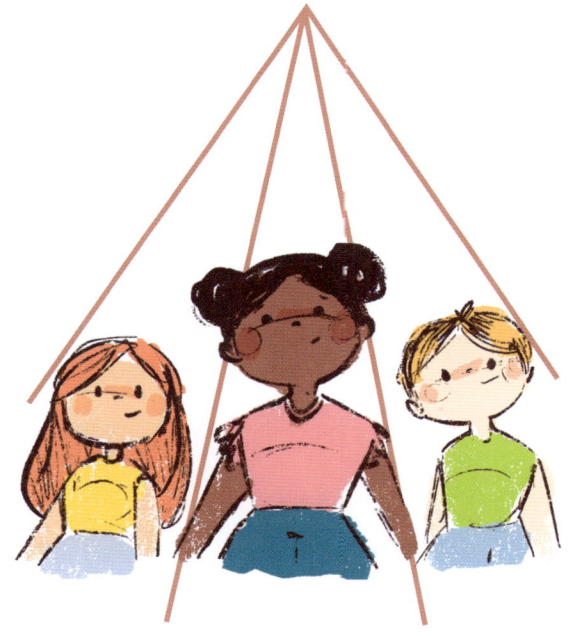

DID YOU NOTICE ALL THE V SHAPES?

All you have to do is make sure your objects or characters fit into a V and you'll have created an extreme camera angle.

JUST A LIL' PERSPECTIVE

PRACTICE TIME

YOU'VE GOT THIS! FINISH MY DRAWING USING TWO-POINT PERSPECTIVE.

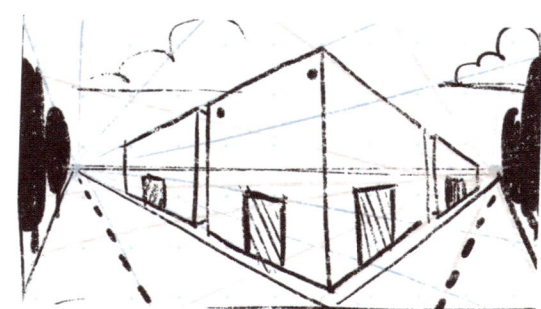

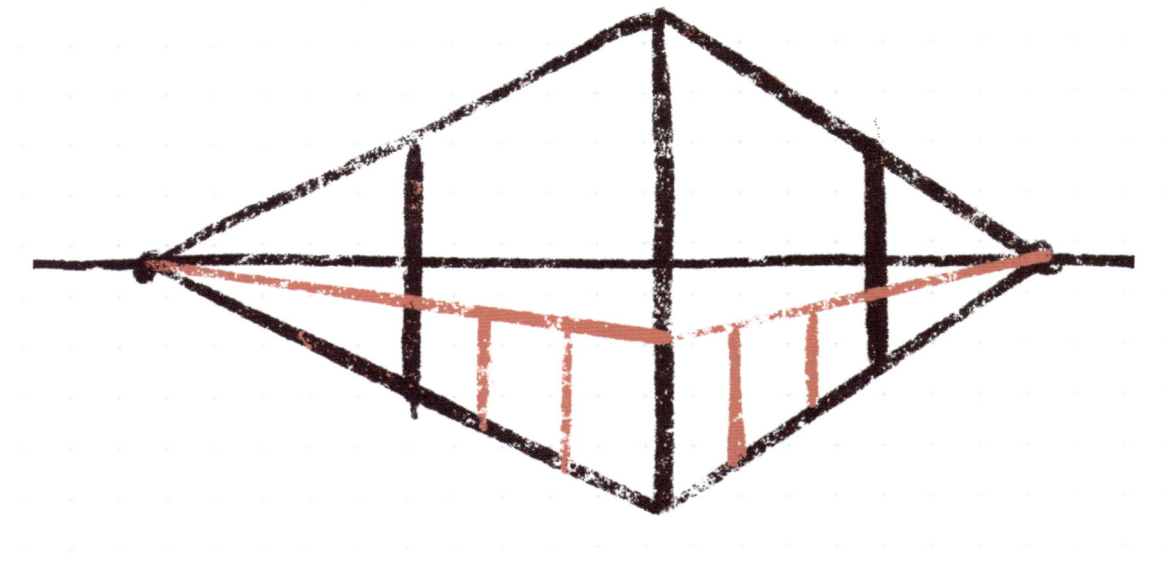

USE THE V SHAPE TO DRAW AN OBJECT OR CHARACTER FROM AN EXTREME CAMERA ANGLE.

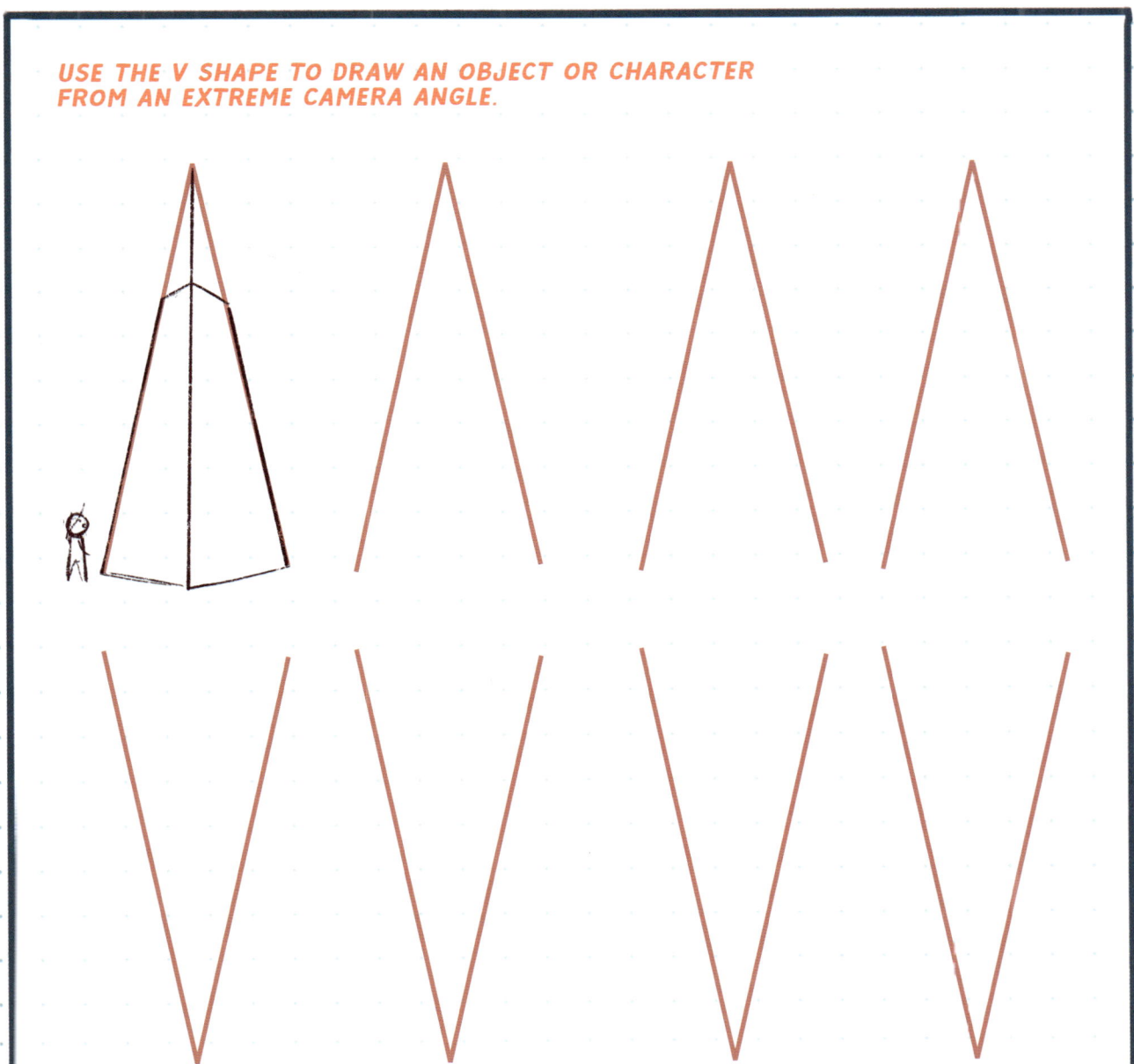

JUST A LIL' PERSPECTIVE 89

my unpopular opinions about perspective

The thing I find artists (including myself) get the most frustrated with when it comes to perspective is that it's tricky to make it perfect. But who said it has to be perfect?

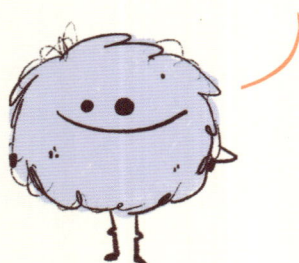

imperfections are still welcome here

LET'S TALK STYLE

Your perspective, just like anything else you draw, can have style. I'll be honest, I love wonky perspective and it fits with my overall style.

I learned how to draw realistic perspective with the ruler and a T square and a grid.

When I use perspective in my art now, I eyeball the lines to a vanishing point and leave my ruler in the drawer.

So take some time to practice perspective and understand how it works and decide how perfect you need it to be for your style from then on.

It's called learning the rules so you can break them.

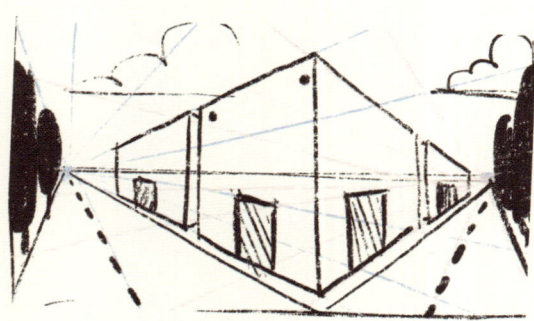

this is okay

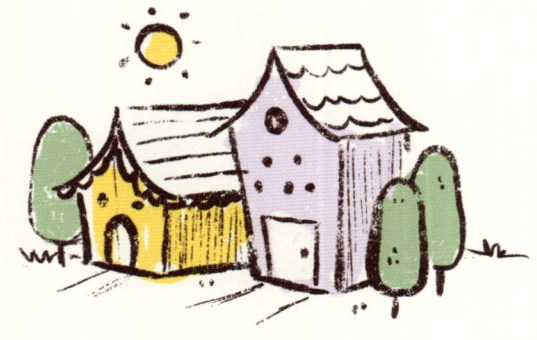

this is, too

BE CONSISTENT AND INTENTIONAL

Whatever style you choose, make sure you're consistent. If your perspective is half perfect and half wonky, it might feel like you messed up. Or if your illustration is very tightly drawn and only the perspective is off or wonky, it'll feel like the wonkiness is an accident.

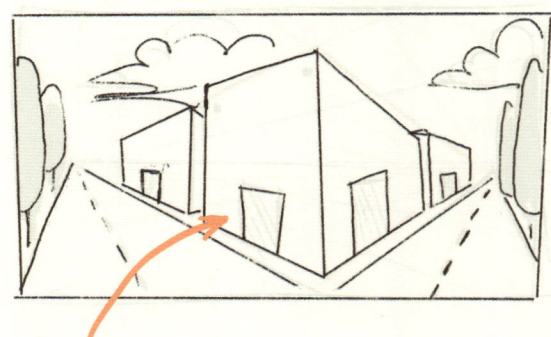

this feels unfinished or accidental

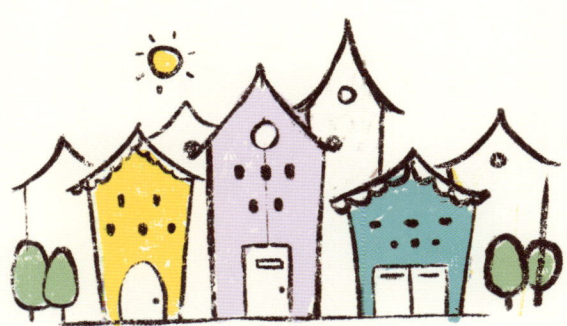

let's give some love to flat drawing styles, too

OR DON'T USE IT AT ALL

Who said you have to use perspective anyway? Draw what you want! Learn perspective if it helps you communicate your ideas better, or stick to the isometric perspective or a flat drawing style.

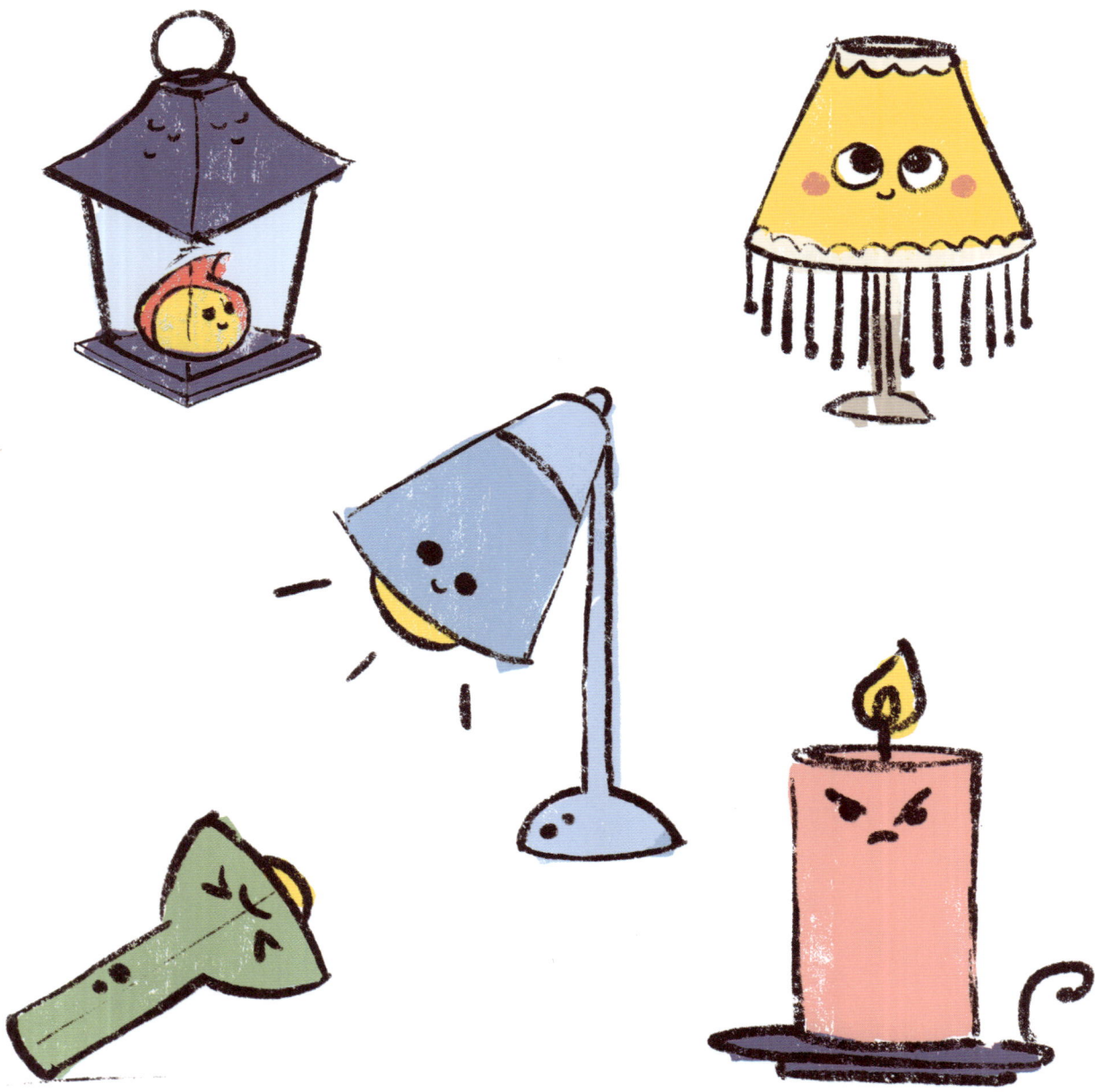

LET'S ADD VALUE

I THINK LIGHT AND SHADOW IS WHAT MAKES ART MAGICAL.

There is something so exciting about taking a drawing and adding light and shadow to it to find it suddenly feels like it lives in its own little world. But even if you're not using light and shadow, you are using values, no matter what you create. When you draw with pencil on a white piece of paper you are using different values (light paper versus dark pencil). Without a difference in values, you wouldn't be able to see . . . anything (white on white is invisible basically). So understanding value is truly a skill every artist should master regardless of the style they use.

Ready to have me shine some light on this for you? Let's go!

why we need value

Value is how light or dark something is. By using different values you can do some pretty cool things in art! If you're not using them well, you might be making your drawing hard to see and understand!

different values

VALUE IS NEEDED TO SEE . . . ANYTHING

If there's not enough difference between your values, it might make it hard to see what you drew. The difference in values creates contrast.

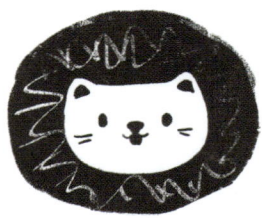 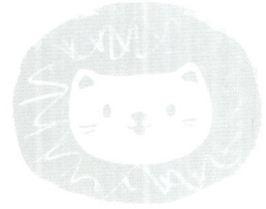

values far apart values close together

CREATE VOLUME

Light and shadow can be used to make an otherwise flat shape appear round.

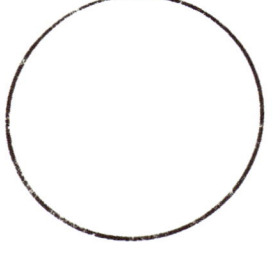 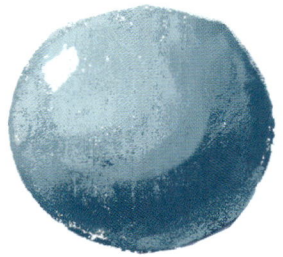

no volume volume

CREATING FOCAL POINTS

Our eyes are drawn to areas that have the most contrast first. So by intentionally making some areas low contrast, and other areas high contrast, you can control where people look.

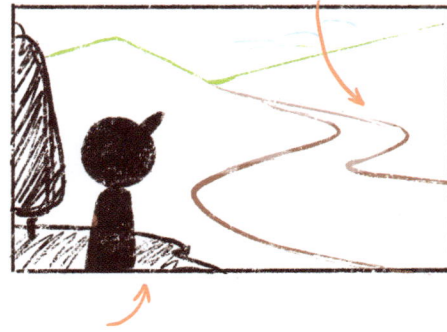

low contrast fades away

high contrast grabs your attention

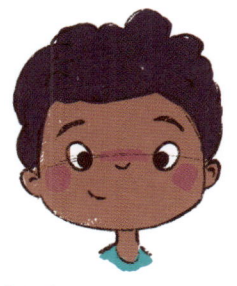

highest contrast in his eyes

WITH OBJECTS AND PEOPLE, TOO

One reason we feel drawn to people's eyes is because of the whites of the eyes contrasted with the darkness of the pupils.

CREATING A MOOD

Light and shadow can also make us *feel* things. For example, lighting from below can feel unnatural and spooky!

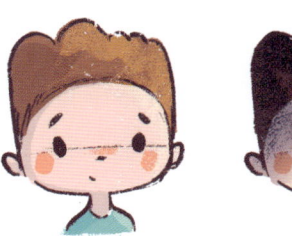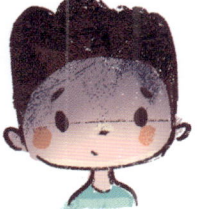

regular versus spooky

LET'S ADD VALUE 95

simple lighting

If you are using light and shadow to create volume, it helps to know what happens when light hits a simple object.

> **did you know?**
> The shadows on the dark side of an object are called form shadows because they create volume! This is separate from a cast shadow that hits a separate object.

LIGHT SOURCE

Let there be light! But it had to come from somewhere, right? This can be the sun or a light bulb or even the moon!

MIDTONE

Right between the light and dark is the middle, so we call that the midtone!

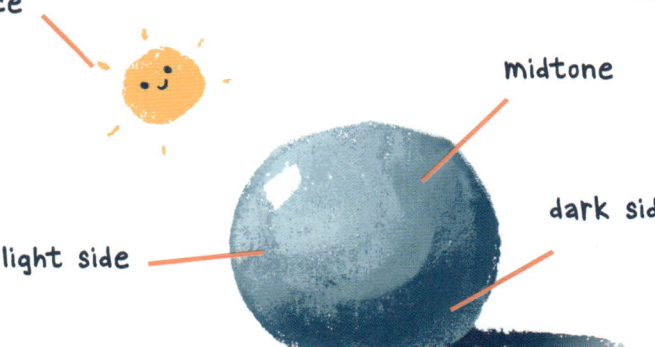

DARK SIDE

The area farthest away from light will be dark. (I've also heard they sometimes have cookies.)

LIGHT SIDE

The area closest to the light source is the light side. On the light side you might see a highlight, which is the bright shiny bit.

CAST SHADOW

This shows us that the light is being blocked by something (in this case, the ball). And so a shadow is cast onto another object (like the ground).

WITH A SQUARE

Here's how this kind of lighting looks on a square. Here the light side, midtone, and dark side are on a different face of the cube.

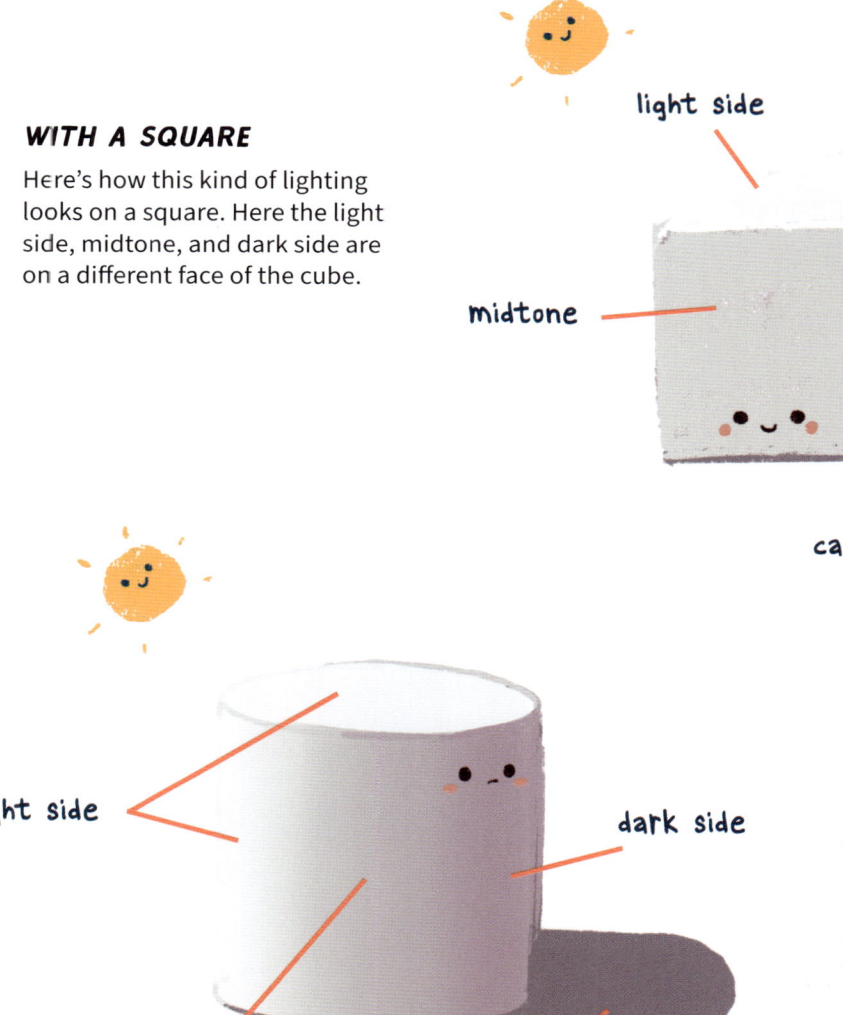

WITH A TUBE

And here's what that looks like on a tube! The tricky part here is the slow change between light and dark on the round side of the tube.

LET'S ADD VALUE **97**

SHADOWS BASED ON SHAPE

Now that you know how shadows work on different shapes, all you have to do is apply each shadow type to the simple shapes in your drawing.

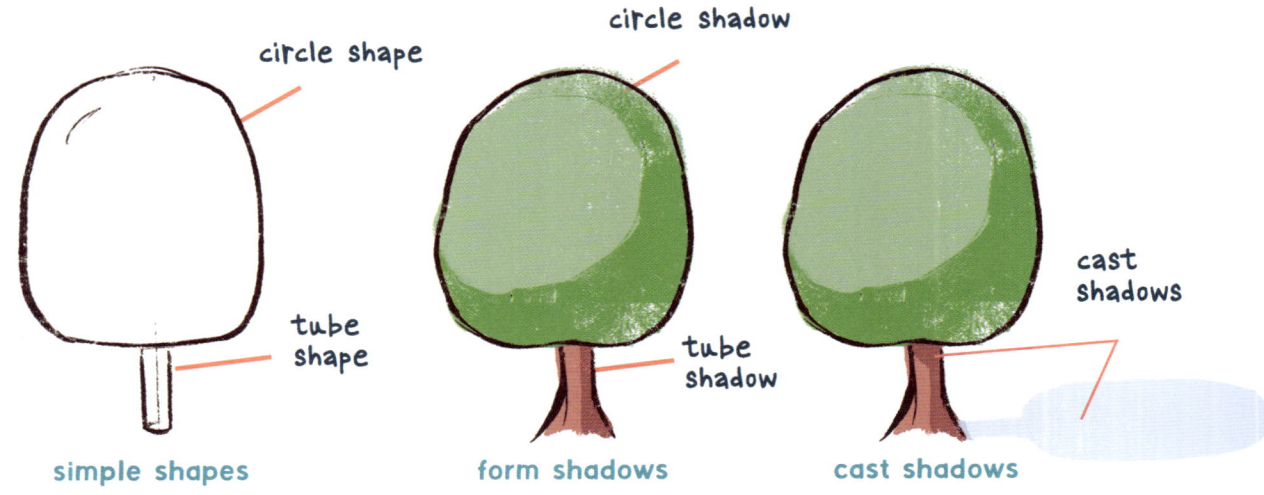

LIGHT SOURCES

As your light source moves, your shadows will move, too. Just like your own shadow does as the day gets longer.

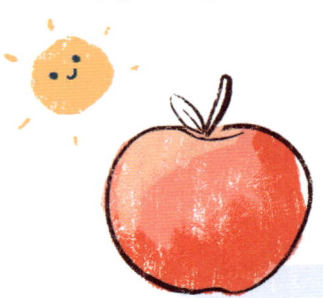
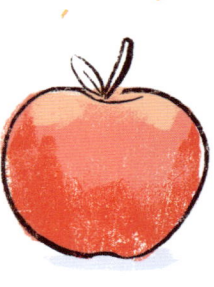
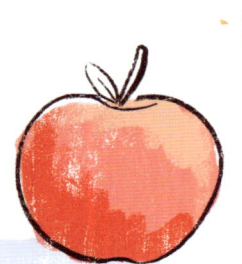

getting edgy with it

Did you know some shadows have harder or sharper edges than others? By adjusting your edges you can create a personal style or be more true to life.

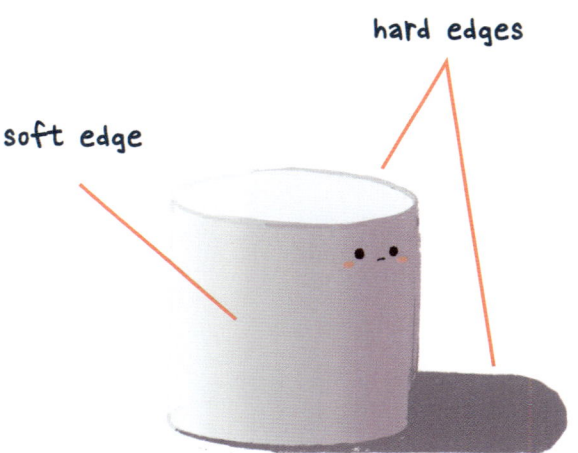

SOFT EDGES

Shadows created from an object slowly getting farther away from the light usually have a soft edge. This is especially true with round objects.

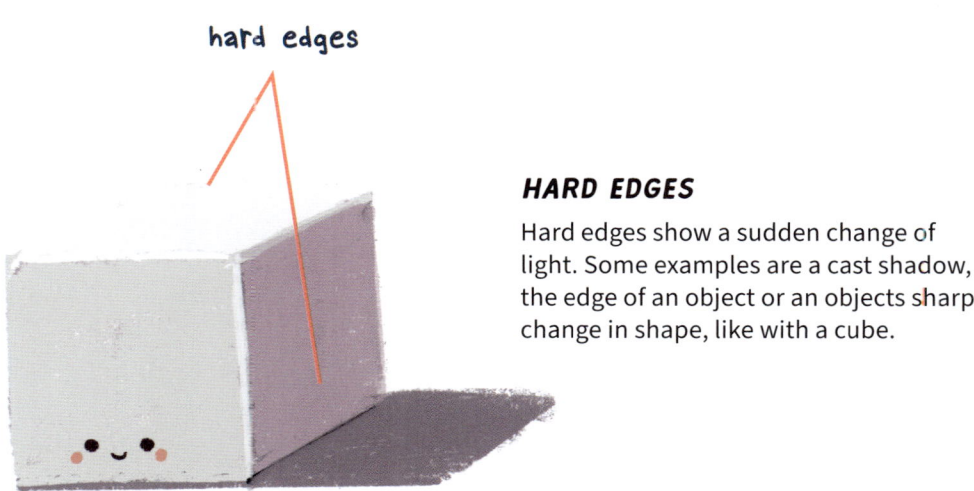

HARD EDGES

Hard edges show a sudden change of light. Some examples are a cast shadow, the edge of an object or an objects sharp change in shape, like with a cube.

shading styles

There's more than one way to shade a ball. Here's some popular methods for creating shadow!

> **tip!**
> To cover a larger area at a time, try using the side of your pencil instead of the tip!

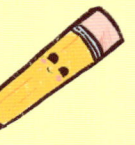

SINGLE LINES

When drawing, I'll often use lines to place the shadows. The closer and thicker the lines are, the darker it will look. You can have them curve to match the shape of your object.

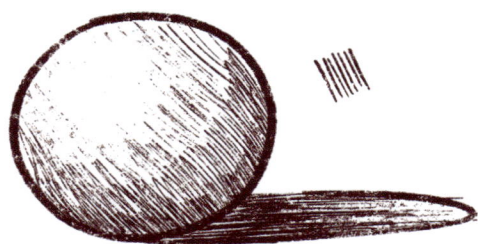

CROSSHATCHING

A very common way of shading with a pen or pencil is to use crosshatching. Instead of single lines, you have the lines cross each other. It's very effective: I don't know why I don't use it.

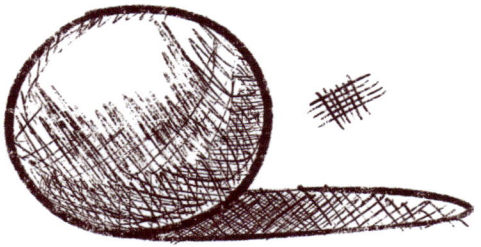

SOFT BLENDING OR SMUDGING

There are a lot more ways to shade, but the most popular is to smudge the pencil after laying it down. You can use a finger (but that's messy). So I suggest a blending stump or Q-tip.

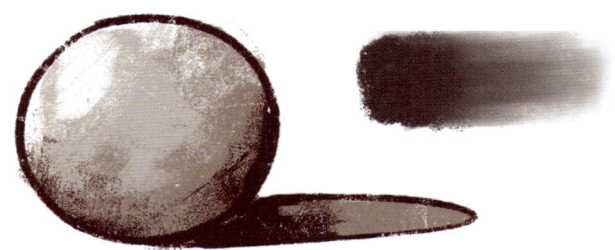

lighting styles

There are lots of drawing styles out there, and not all of them include light and shadow. Here's a few examples of styles with different light and shadow choices.

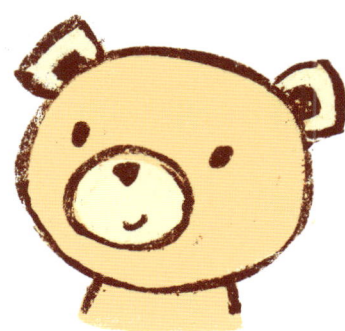

values only

VALUES ONLY

Here's an example of a drawing style that uses only different values for clarity and doesn't use shadows and light.

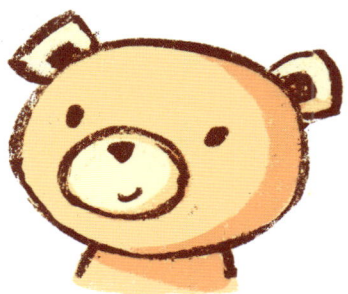

hard shadows only

HARD SHADOWS ONLY

A really common drawing style uses only hard shadow shapes (so no soft edges) to create form. This is a personal fave of mine.

FULL LIGHTING

Or you can choose to use a full lighting style with hard and soft shadows, as well as a light side, a midtone, and a dark side.

which style do you like best?

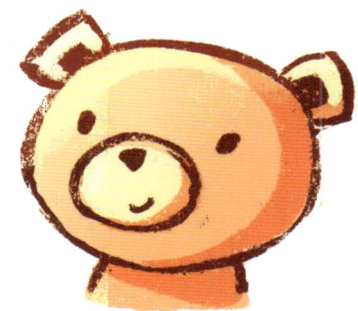

full light and shadow

LET'S ADD VALUE

PRACTICE TIME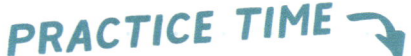

CAN YOU TELL ME WHERE THE LIGHT SOURCE IS COMING FROM? USE AN ARROW TO SHOW THE DIRECTION OF THE LIGHT.

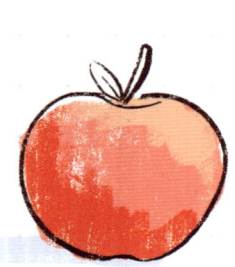
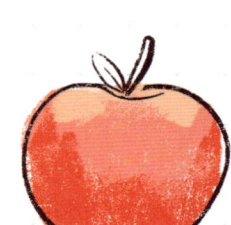
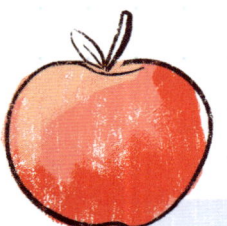

NOW TRY YOUR OWN.

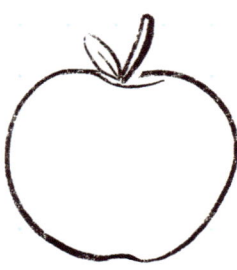
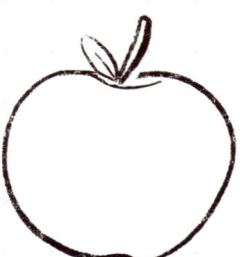
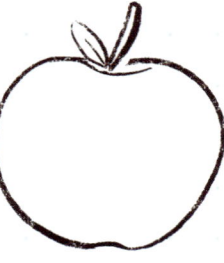

TRY DIFFERENT SHADING METHODS:

SINGLE LINES **CROSSHATCHING** **BLENDING**

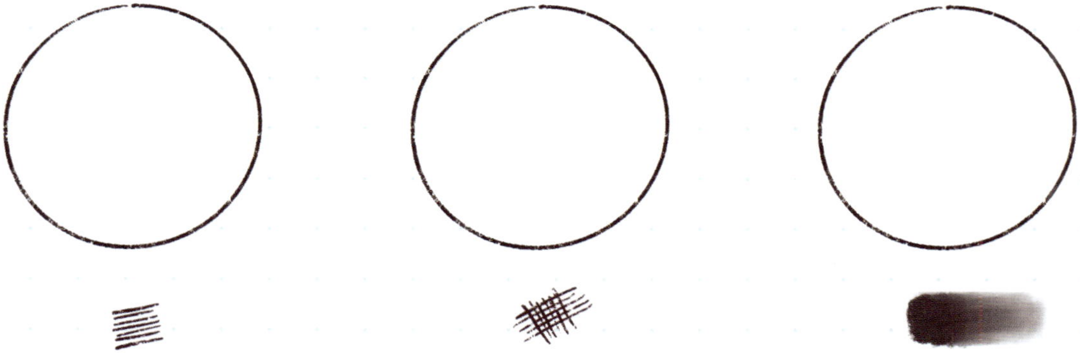

PRACTICE SHADING THESE SHAPES—YOU CHOOSE THE LIGHT SOURCE.

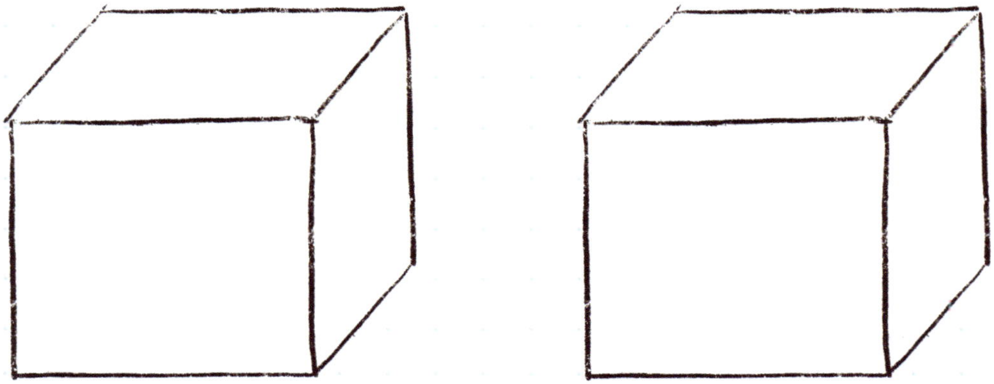

LET'S ADD VALUE

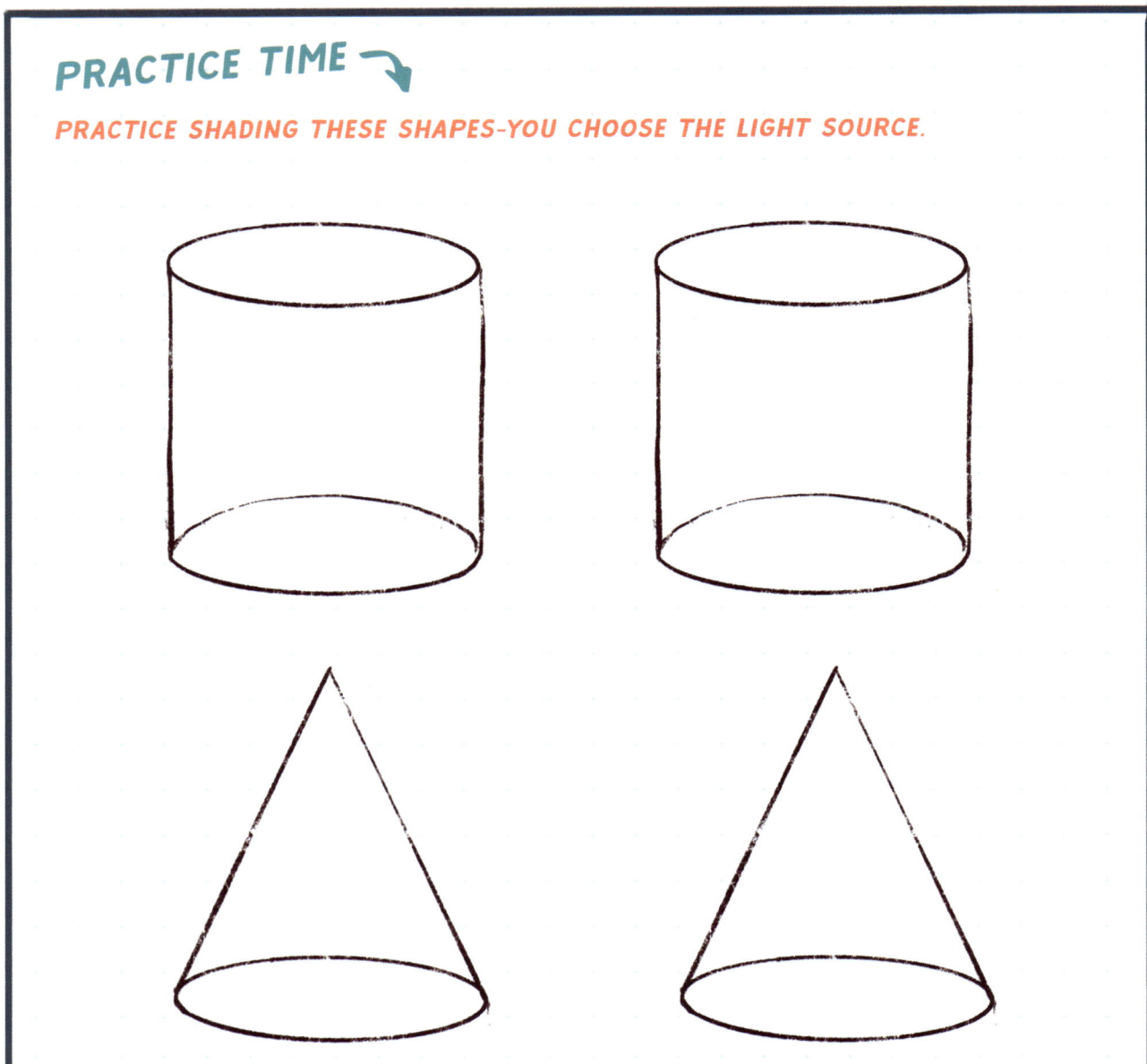

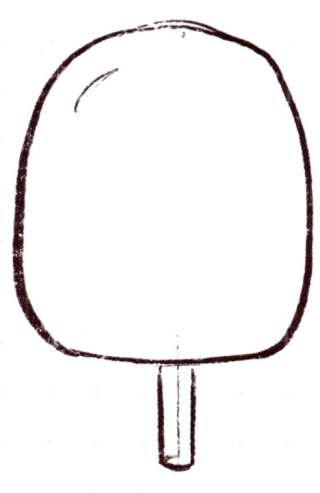
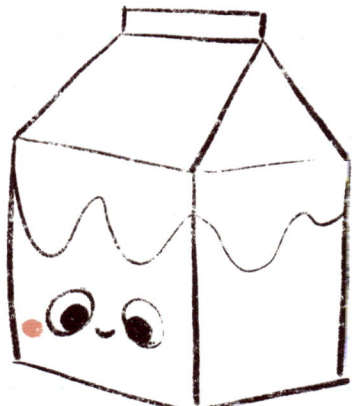

NOW YOU DRAW AN OBJECT AND LIGHT IT.

LET'S ADD VALUE

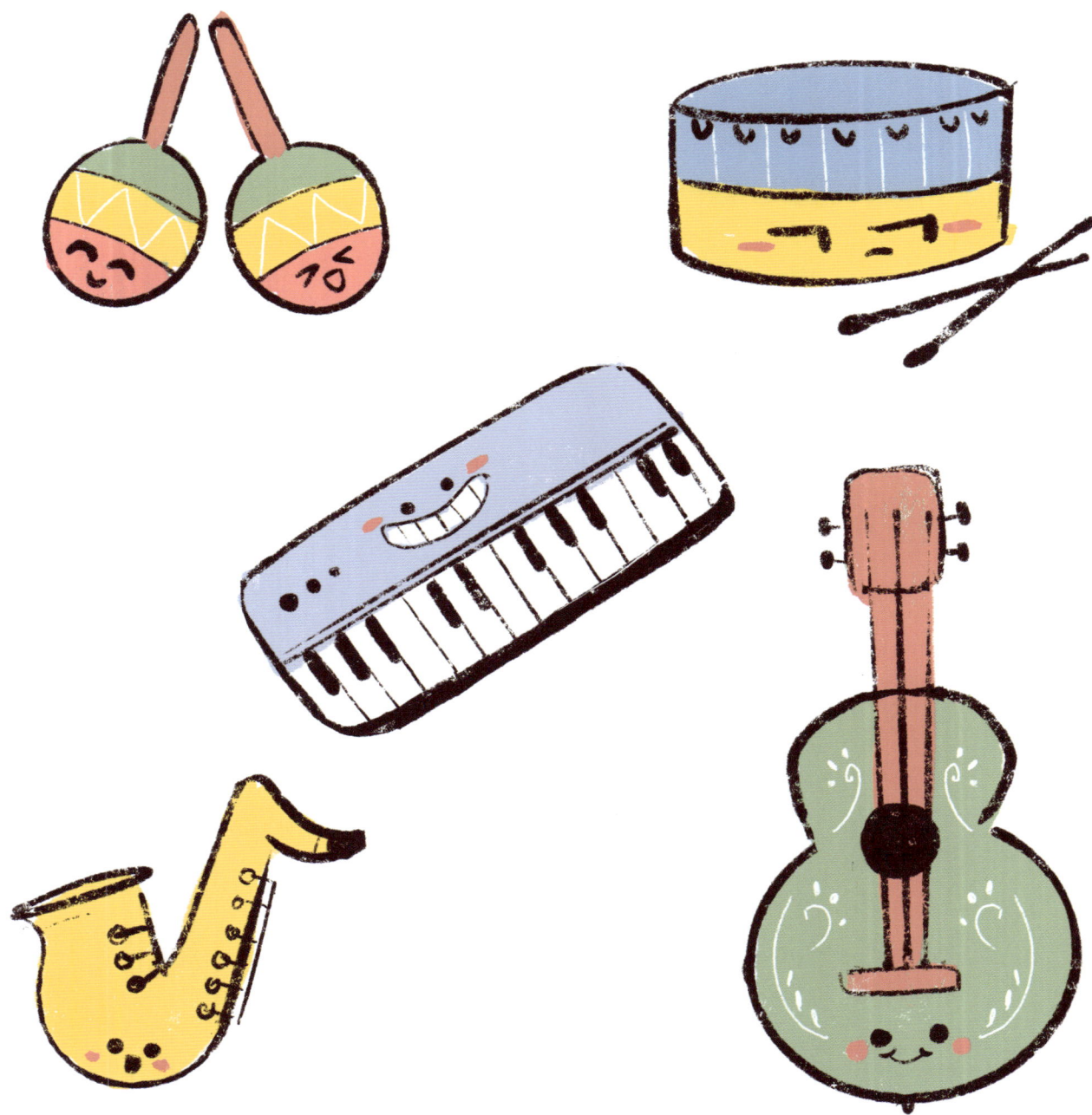

COMPOSING YOUR ART

IF YOU WANT TO DRAW MORE THAN ONE OBJECT TOGETHER, YOU'LL WANT TO KNOW A LITTLE BIT ABOUT COMPOSITION.

Composition is all about the placement of things in a space. The idea is to organize all these things in a way that is nice to look at or helps you communicate an idea. I like to think of it like organizing my room. If there's a lot of clutter, it's hard to even know what to look at when I walk in. But if everything is put where it goes and my bed is made, I walk in, look at my big beautiful bed (since it's the biggest thing in the room) and breathe a sigh of relief! In your drawings you can use composition to make it easier on the viewer, but you can also use it to tell a story. Maybe you WANT the person to feel overwhelmed rather than relaxed when they look at what you drew. By using your knowledge of composition, you can control what people look at and what you want to communicate.

let me see your thumbs

Not the ones on your hands, you silly goose! A thumb, or thumbnail, is a tiny sketch that artists use to plan a drawing out. They're great because you can make the mistakes you want here AND come up with great ideas too!

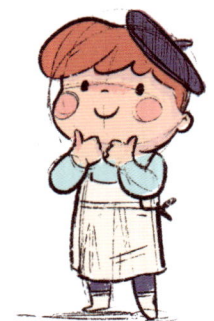

SIZE MATTERS

If you are drawing traditionally, I recommend no more than a one-inch size. It's super important that they are small so you don't start working on details too soon.

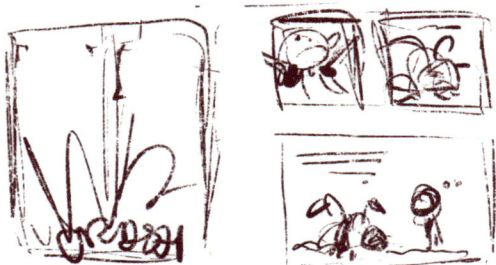

this is the actual size of my sketches

A NOTE FOR DIGITAL ARTISTS

Although I work digitally most of the time, I find hand-drawn thumbnails to be much better. Digital art makes it too easy for you to undo or zoom in. I work with a pen or pencil and just photograph and upload the one I like when I'm done.

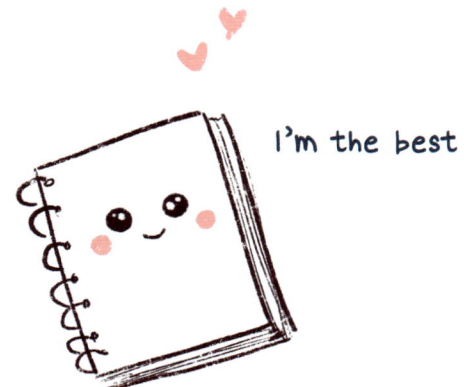

I'm the best

focal points

A focal point is the area that you look at first. It draws your eye to it.

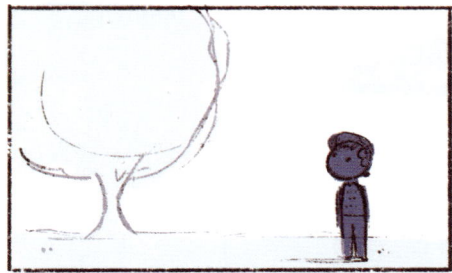

eye drawn to the person

USE VALUE

One of the main ways to create a focal point is by using value to create contrast.

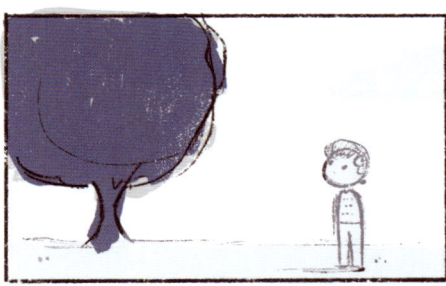

eye drawn to the tree

SECONDARY FOCAL POINTS

You can also have a secondary focal point. It's often the area with the next most contrast.

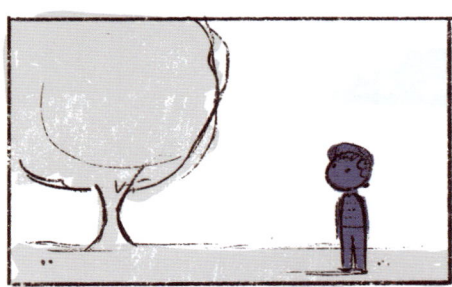

you look at the person, and then the tree

tips for success

I mentioned that focal points are created by using contrast. There is more than one way to create contrast! Here are some things that will assist in creating a focal point.

VALUE

The area where you have the darkest dark up against your lightest light will create contrast. This can also be something white over a dark area.

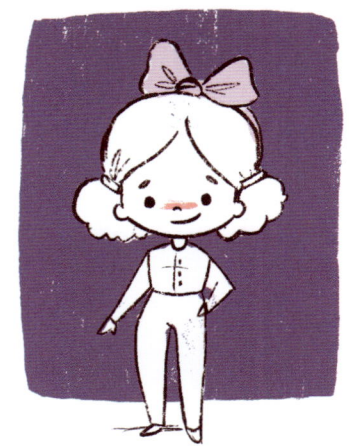

COLOR

Often warm and vibrant colors pop forward, while muted and cool colors fade back.

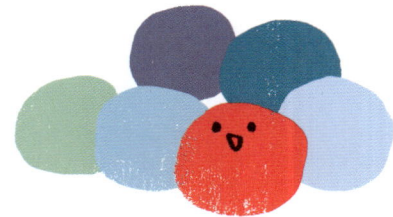

focal point

THE RULE OF THIRDS

Rules are meant to be broken, but the rule of thirds is a very popular way to place your focal point. It allows a lot of room for your eye to enjoy the page.

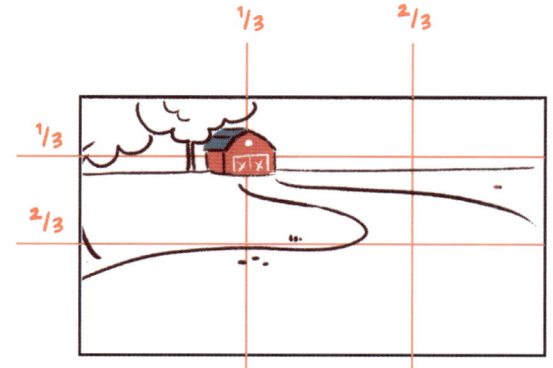

USE A SPIRAL

It can be very pleasing to use a spiral shape like this to create movement in your art. This helps lead the eye all around your image instead of getting stuck in one or two spots.

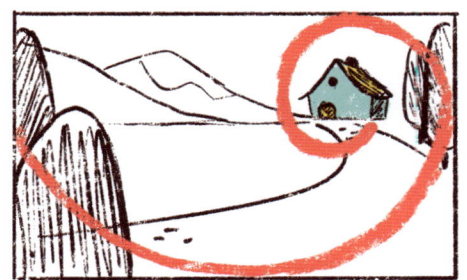

WHEN TO KEEP IT CENTERED?

There might be times that you don't want lots of movement in your art. In that case you would put your focal point right in the center. Try this if you want something to be easier to read, feel frozen, or feel more formal.

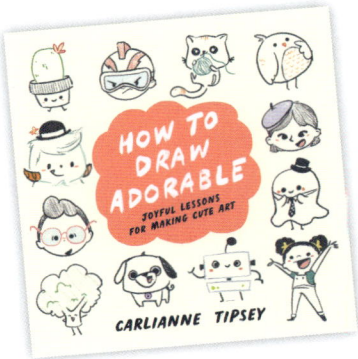

FRAMING DEVICES

By adding elements to the sides of the drawing, it helps keep your eyes within the drawing.

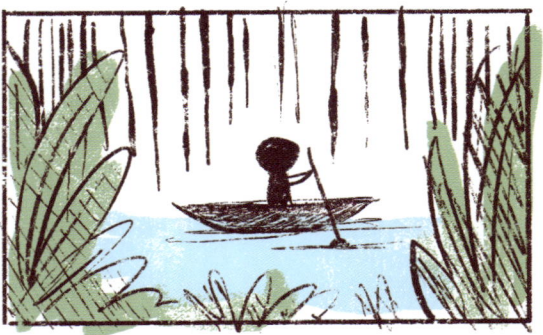

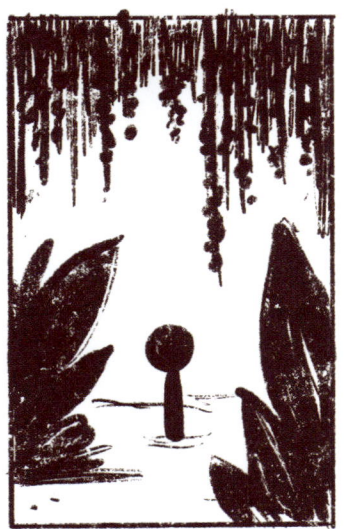

FOREGROUND, BACKGROUND, MIDDLE GROUND

Another way to add framing devices is through the introduction of a foreground! Having a foreground, middle ground, and background in a drawing adds a lot of depth, too!

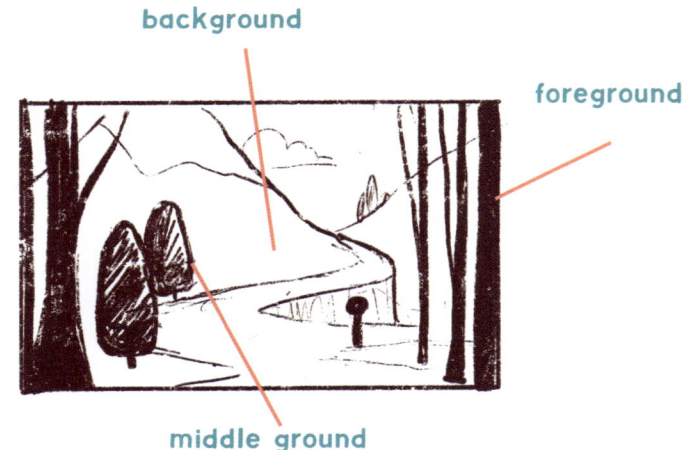

LEADING LINES

The direction of the lines you create in your drawing can also be used to direct the eye. For example, in this drawing I use the leaves to keep your eye moving around the image and looking at the fairy.

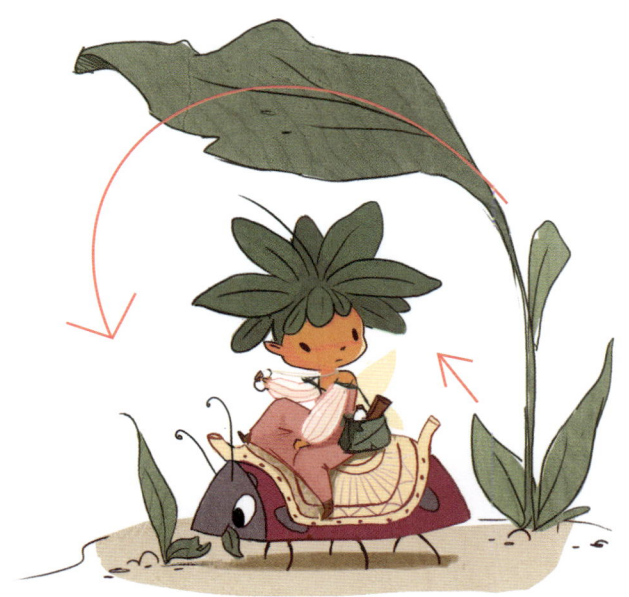

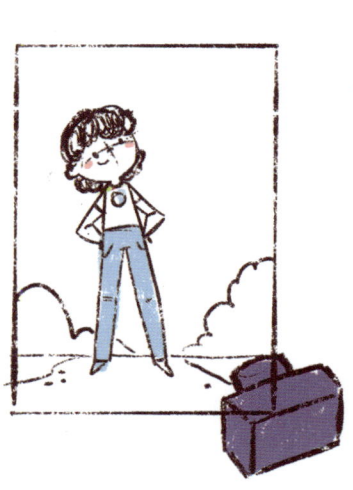

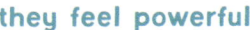

they feel powerful

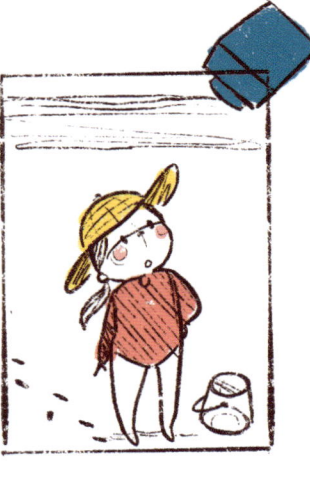

she feels small

CHANGE UP THE MOOD

One way to show a variety of emotions in your art is to try out different camera angles.

COMPOSING YOUR ART 113

masterful compositions

Why not use the compositions that the great masters have been using for centuries? Here are some of my faves and the feels they give me.

COMPOSITIONS AND SAMPLES

I'll share a popular composition on the left and an example of it in on the right.

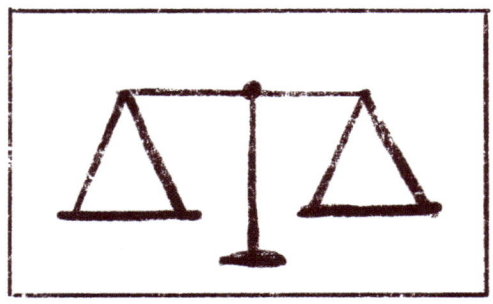

symmetrical

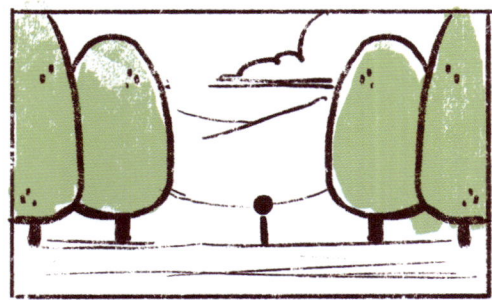

feels peaceful

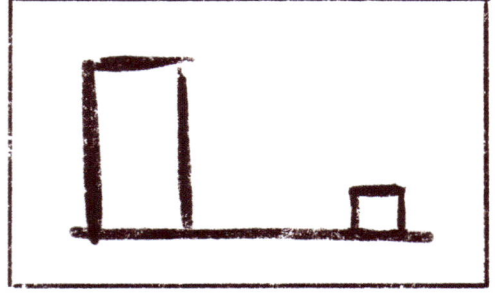

asymmetrical

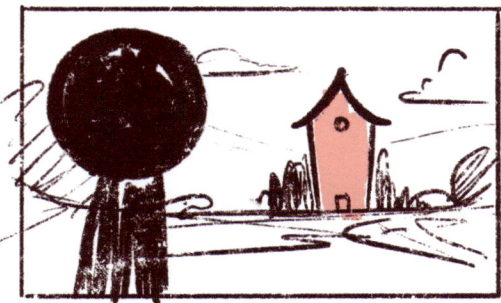

feels interesting

radiating

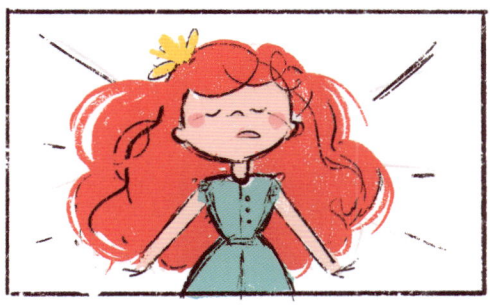
lots of energy

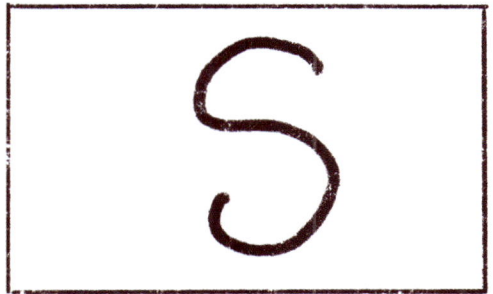
S shaped

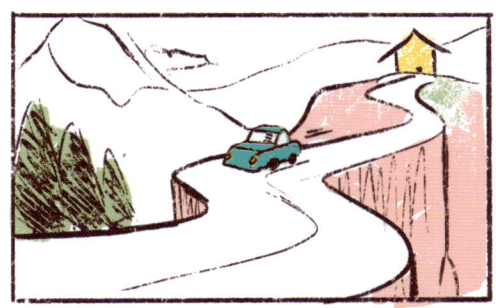
draws your eye

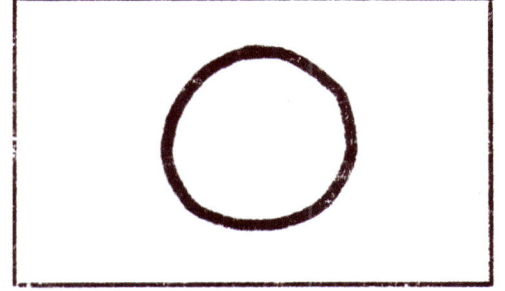
O shaped

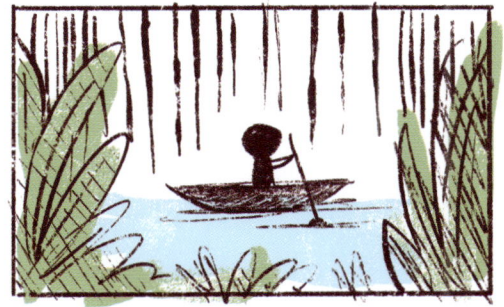
feels private

COMPOSING YOUR ART 115

pump up the story

You can also try changing how far the viewer is from your subject. This is super common in movies where they move the camera to create different feelings.

FAR-AWAY SHOTS

When the camera is far away from your subject, it can be used just to help set up the scene so where we see things are, but it can also make the scene feel quiet or lonely.

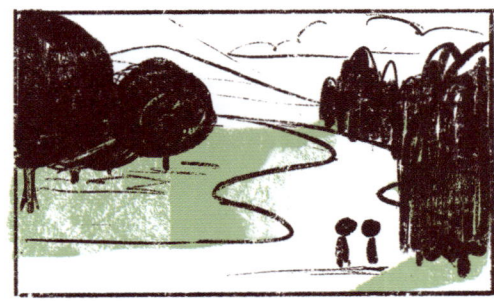

focus on location

CLOSE-UPS

Close-up shots can help us really see and experience the emotion of the character, or to get clarity on an object.

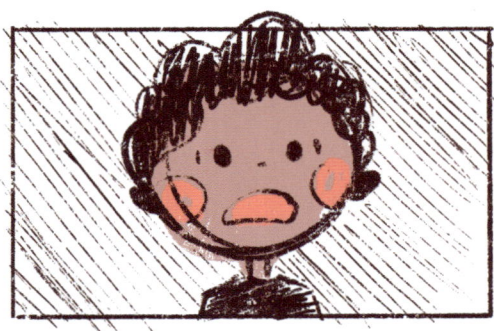

focus on emotion

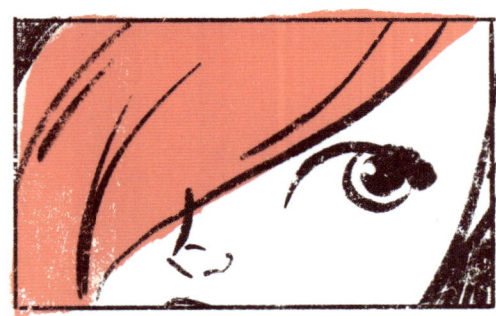

added intensity

LOW CAMERA

When the camera is below a character, it makes them feel powerful and strong or creates a feeling of hope.

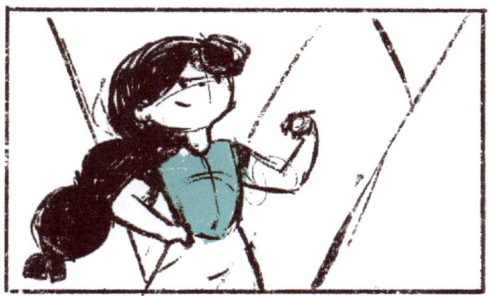

powerful

HIGH CAMERA

If the camera is above, it can make whatever we are looking at feel weak or small.

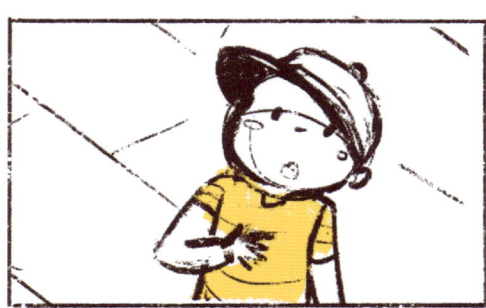

feels small

TILTED CAMERA

A tilted camera angle is super high energy. It can feel exciting or dangerous. I love when this angle gets pulled out during a car chase scene. This is also called a dutch angle.

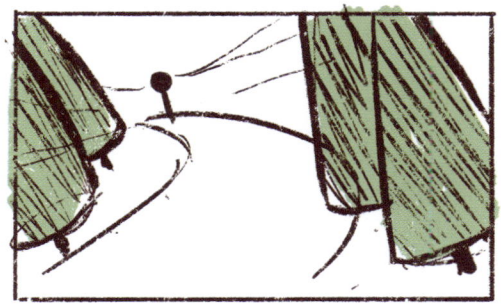

high energy

COMPOSING YOUR ART

PRACTICE TIME ↴

TRY OUT SOME COMPOSITIONS (IDEA: A PERSON AND A TREE).

SYMMETRICAL

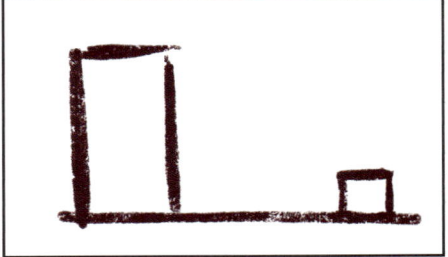 

ASYMMETRICAL

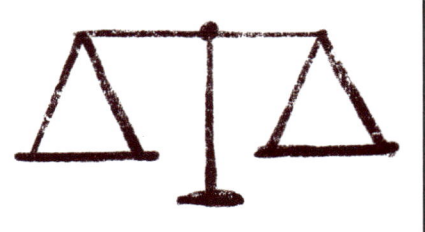 

RADIATING

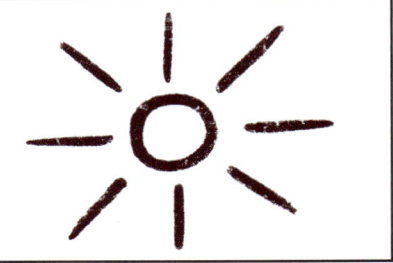 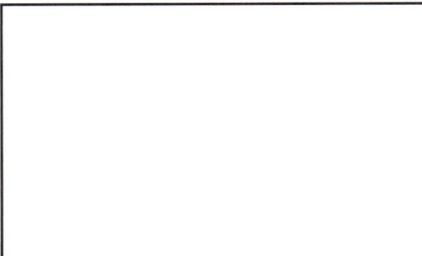

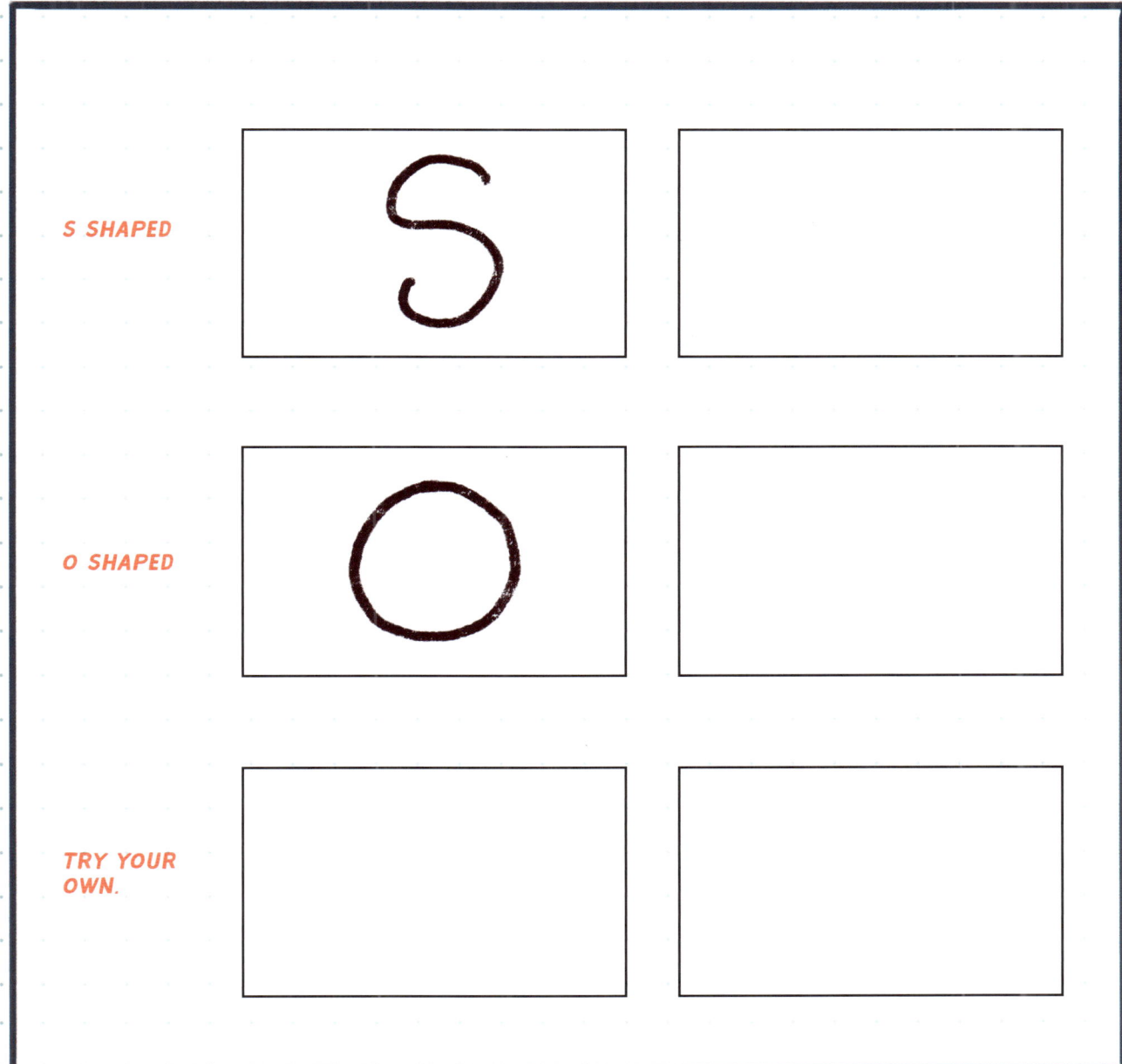

COMPOSING YOUR ART 119

PRACTICE TIME ↘

TRY OUT SOME CAMERA ANGLES.

FAR-AWAY

CLOSE-UP

EXTREME CLOSE-UP

LOW CAMERA

HIGH CAMERA

TILTED CAMERA

COMPOSING YOUR ART **121**

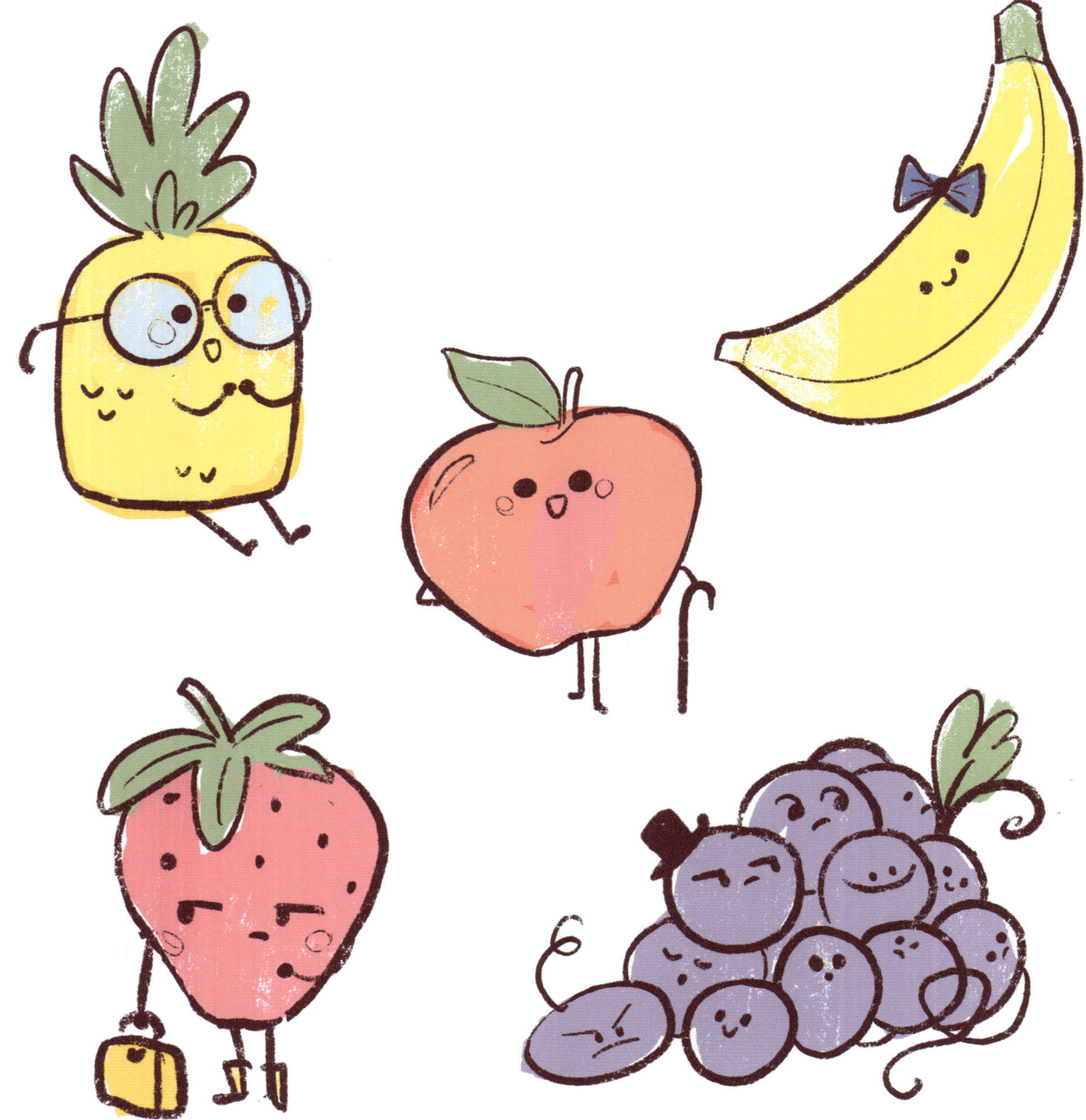

CHARACTERS ANYONE CAN DRAW

I HAD TO PUT THIS CHAPTER IN HERE, BECAUSE THEY'RE MY FAVORITE THING TO DRAW.

Drawing characters can feel tricky, but it's just because we are super familiar with what a body and face and hands look like. It's literally connected to you at all times. In this chapter I'll teach you a super simple way to draw people and characters. You can take this information and learn more realistic stuff later if you want. However, you don't even need to draw people to draw characters!

Let me show you what I mean.

it's all about personality

Drawing people can be tricky, but that doesn't mean you can't draw characters. Anything can be a character!

STORYTELLING

When you add the elements I'm about to share with you, you'll be adding a little bit of story to your character. This makes them feel more alive!

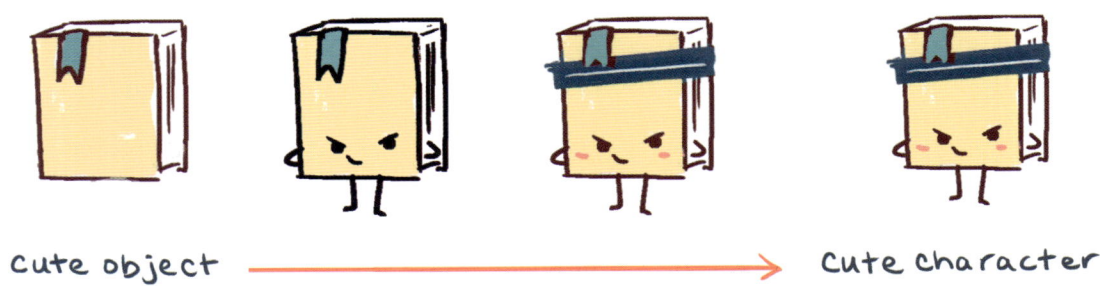

cute object → cute character

PICK A THING

You can choose an object or shape or whatever you want to start with here.

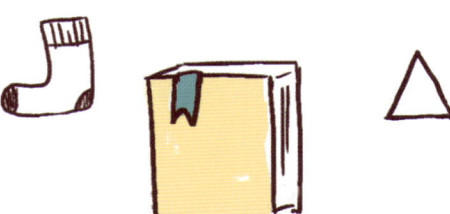

THE CUTEST BEGINNER DRAWING BOOK EVER

ADD SOME FEELS

The first thing that separates something that is alive versus something that's not is emotion. So first up, let's give our object an emotion.

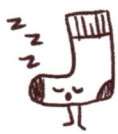 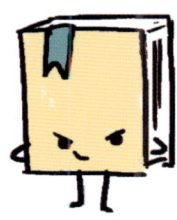

ACCESSORIZE IT

What makes two people with two different styles seem so different? The way we dress or the things we have give us a little hint at our personality.

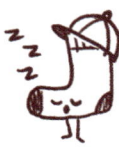  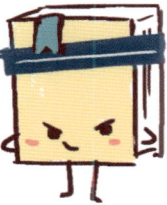

GET MOVIN'

To really make your character feel full of life, you can add some motion or movement.

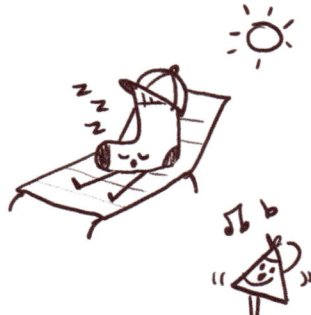 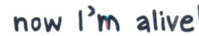 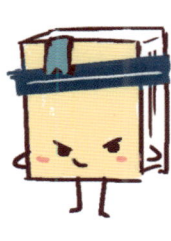

now I'm alive!

get started with people

We don't have to use complex shapes to draw people. Here's a simple method to get started drawing.

STICK FIGURES

You don't need perfect anatomy to draw cute characters! Knowing how to draw a simple stick figure will get you a lot further than you might think. Just pick a stick figure style that works for you.

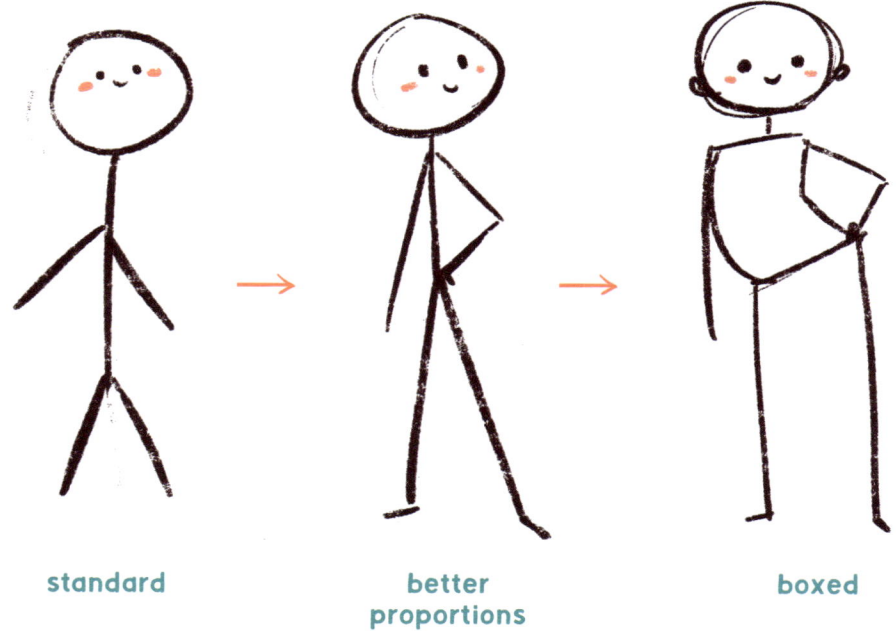

standard → better proportions → boxed

CREATE A CHARACTER

If you use the boxed stick figure, you can add just a few more lines to make limbs, hair, and clothing. With just a bit of cleanup, you've created a simple character!

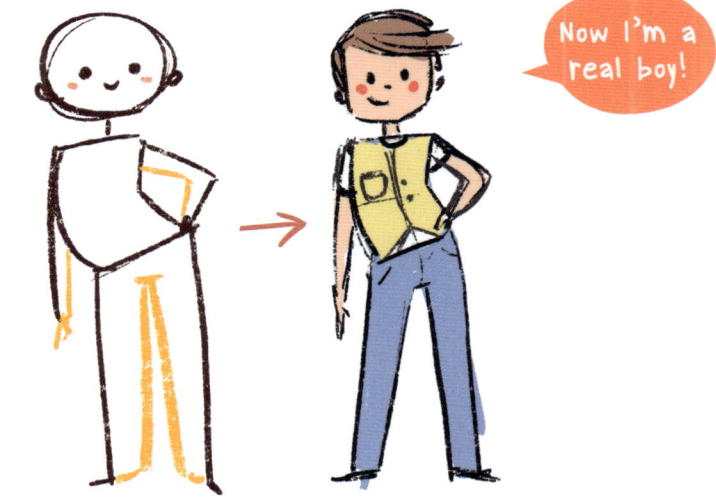

PLAY WITH SHAPES

When you get more advanced you can create more body types by changing your square shape into something else.

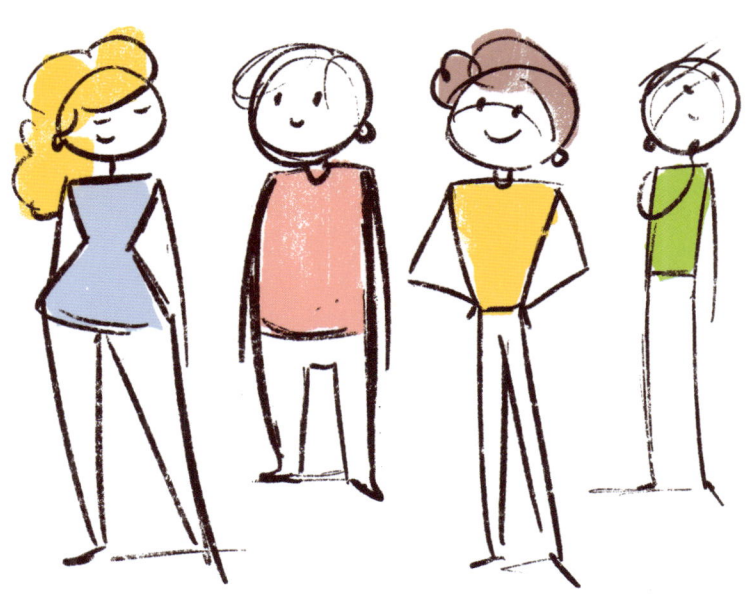

gesture drawing

Gesture drawing is what artists call their rough drawings when sketching people. These sketches are done quickly to get a sense of the character's emotions and body position (also known as their pose). At this stage it's okay to make the pose more dramatic than it might be in real life—it's much easier to dial back an overly expressive pose than it is to add energy to a stiff pose.

KEEP IT SIMPLE, KEEP IT ROUGH!

Don't worry about details or proportions during the early stages of drawing a pose. You can add those later. For now, keep things loosey-goosey and focus on getting the emotions and body positions jusssst right.

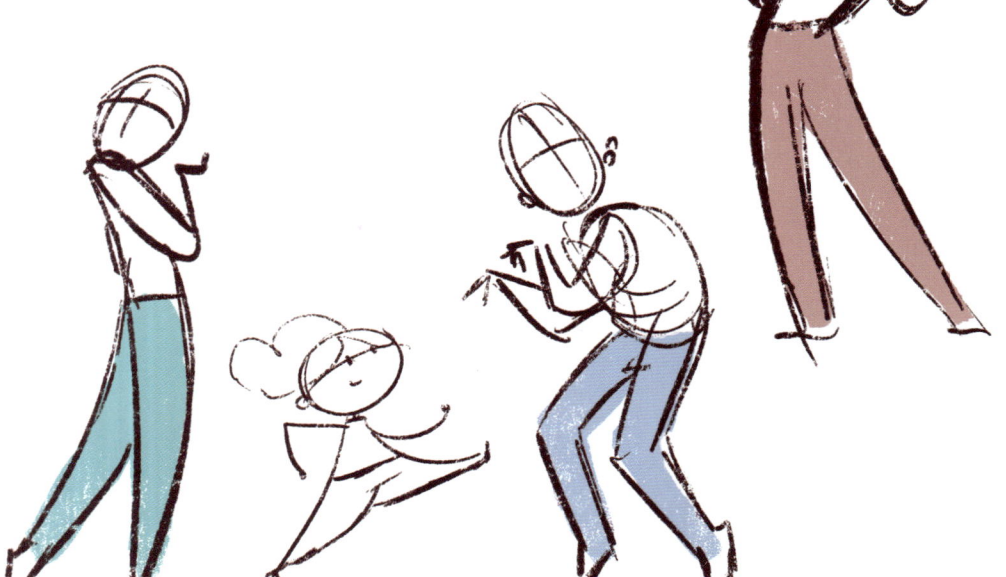
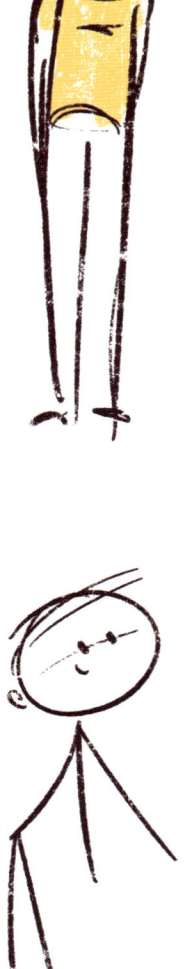

LINE OF ACTION

The line of action is usually a single line that shows the energy or emotion of the character—and is a great base to build on! In some poses, I like to add the head first and then the line of action. It's okay to be flexible!

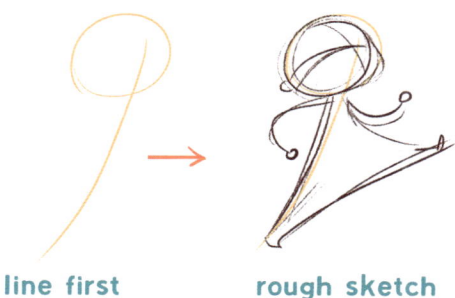

line first   rough sketch

MOVEMENT AND EMOTION

By using the line of action, you can focus on the emotion and movement in the pose. If your line of action is very straight then your pose is likely stiff.

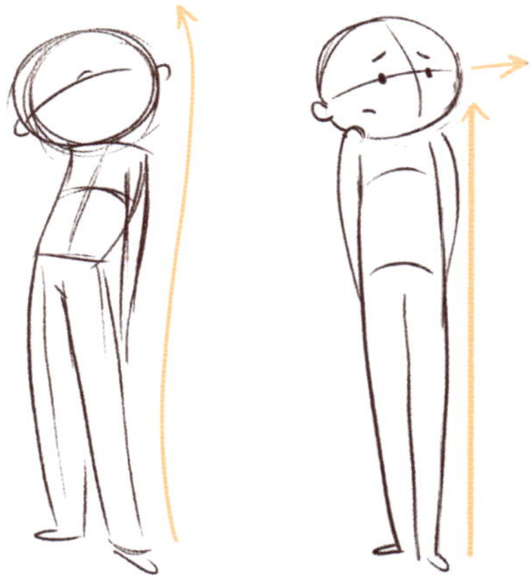

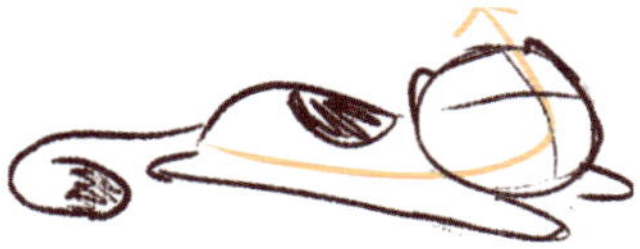

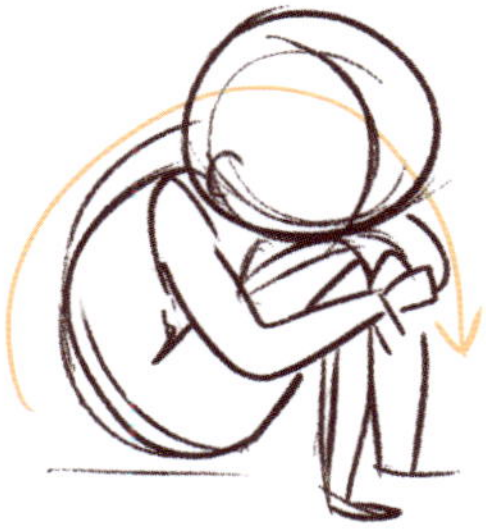

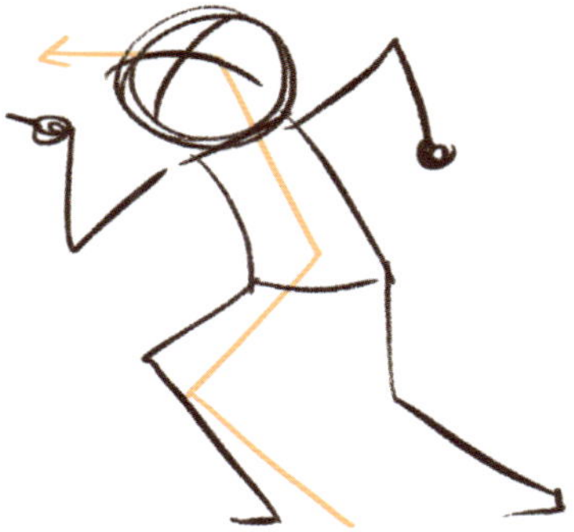

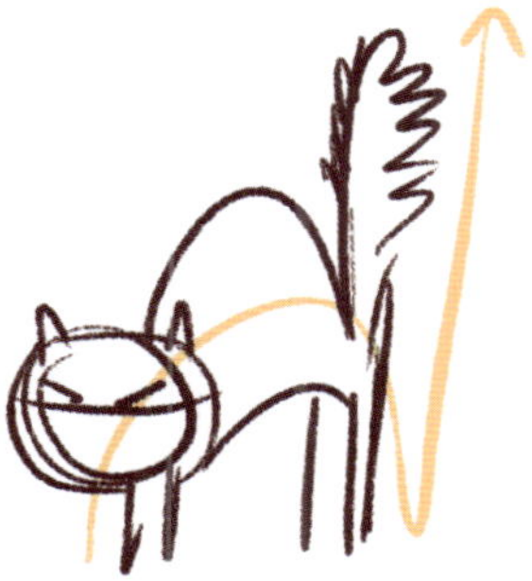

posing tips

Here's a few things I check for when I'm drawing my poses.

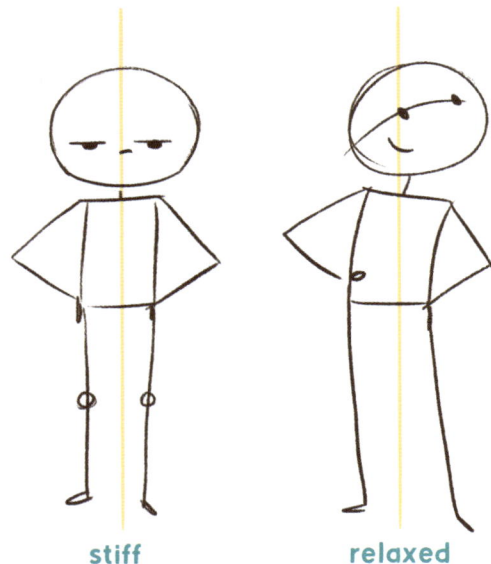

stiff   relaxed

CREATE ASYMMETRY

If you draw down the middle of your character you can check to see if you're using asymmetry in your pose. Symmetrical poses feel more stiff, asymmetrical poses are more relaxed.

USE THE NOSE FOR BALANCE

You nose what is fun? You can make sure your character is balanced by drawing a line down from their nose and making sure they have at least one foot underneath it.

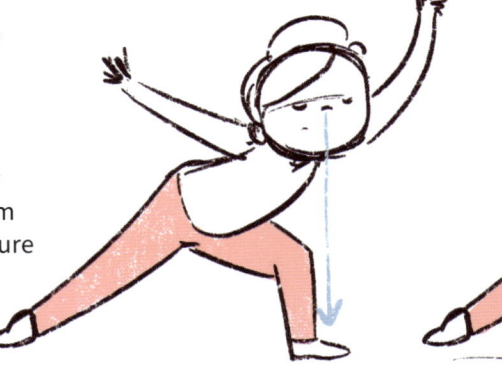
balanced

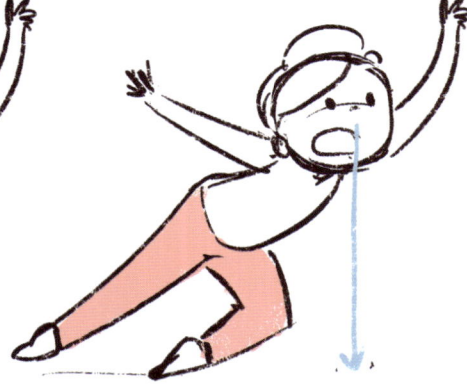
falling over

CONSIDER THE EMOTION

Before I start to clean up my gesture drawing, I check to make sure that my drawing is telling the story and is showing the emotion I wanted to create.

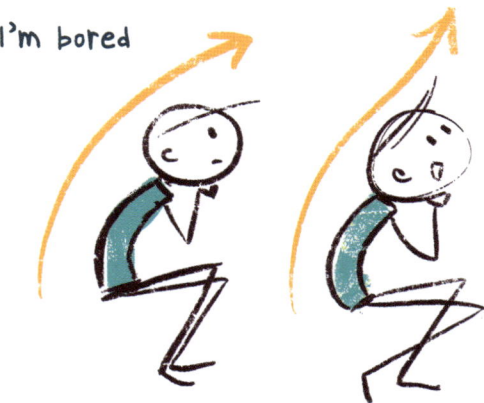

CHECK THE SILHOUETTE

Fill your drawing in with black. The new shape you've made is called a silhouette. If you can understand what is happening in a pose just by the silhouette, then you know your poses will read clearly.

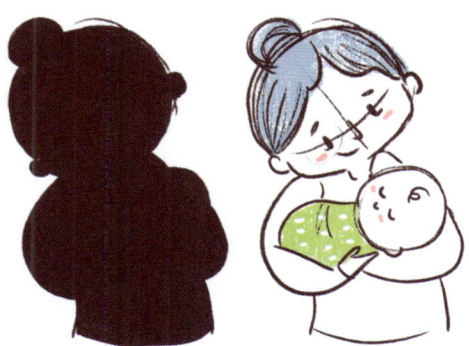

unclear silhouette

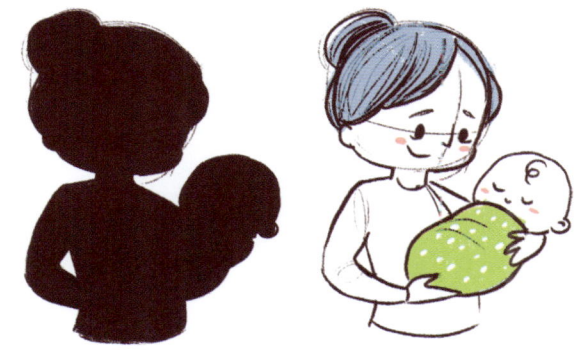

clear silhouette

ellipses are your friend

To help you draw people (who are mostly round shapes, in my opinion), it's really helpful to know a little about ellipses. You can use them to place the eyes on a head or simply understand how to draw bodies a little better.

WHAT'S AN ELLIPSE?

When a circle is in perspective it becomes an oval shape, so to avoid confusion we call them "ellipses." Ellipses are super helpful when drawing round objects, like heads!

THE CIRCLE FLATTENS OUT

Imagine you're looking at a coin lying flat on a table. It's shaped like a full circle, right? But if you pick the coin up and tilt it around, it'll go from looking like a circle to looking flatter and flatter . . . This distortion of the circle as it moves is what we are going to call an ellipse.

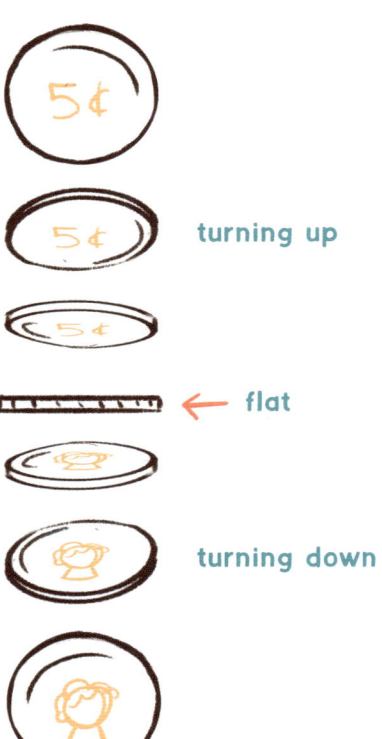

KEEP AN EYE ON THE CURVE

Here's how this might look inside of a tube or a round object like a body or a head! See how the stripes on his shirt slowly get less round?

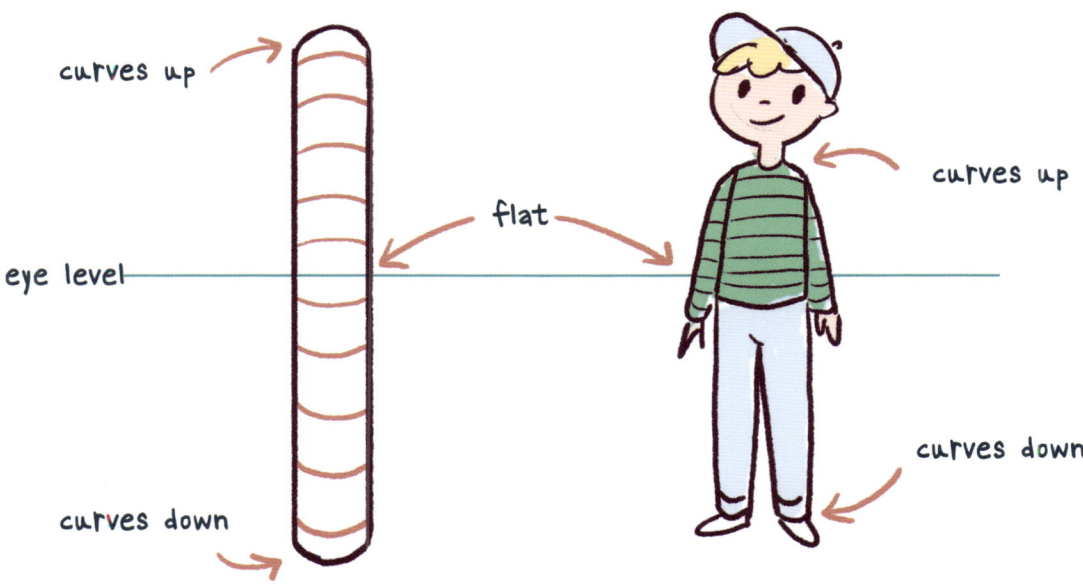

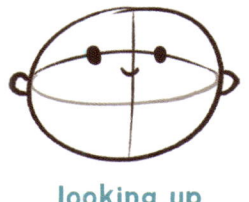
looking up

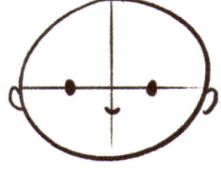
eye level

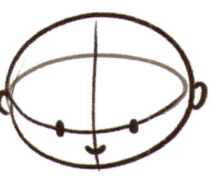
looking down

CHARACTERS ANYONE CAN DRAW

SOME IDEAS FOR YOU

Don't get stuck—get started! Here are some objects, emotions, props, and actions for you to mix, match, and get drawing.

objects

circle
square
coffee cup
tissue box
printer
stamp
leafy plant
shoebox
pillow
ruler
sketchbook

actions

running
jumping
fencing
cooking
weight lifting
eating cotton candy
waving
talking to a friend
skipping rocks
reading a book
sunbathing
swimming

emotions

sad
angry
jealous
anxious
happy
excited
numb
dazed
surprised
shocked
sleepy
sick
determined
confused
furious
mischievous
confident
shy
bored

props

hats
more hats
bows
sneakers
backpack
freckles
glasses
goggles
tie
mustache
scooter
purse
sandwich
umbrella
yoga mat
hair
pink cheeks
eyelashes

134 THE CUTEST BEGINNER DRAWING BOOK EVER

PRACTICE TIME

USE THE IDEAS ON THE LEFT TO DRAW SOME CUTE CHARACTERS.

PRACTICE TIME

DRAW THESE POSES.

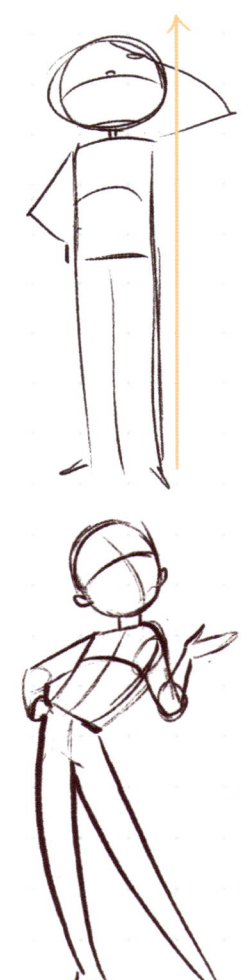

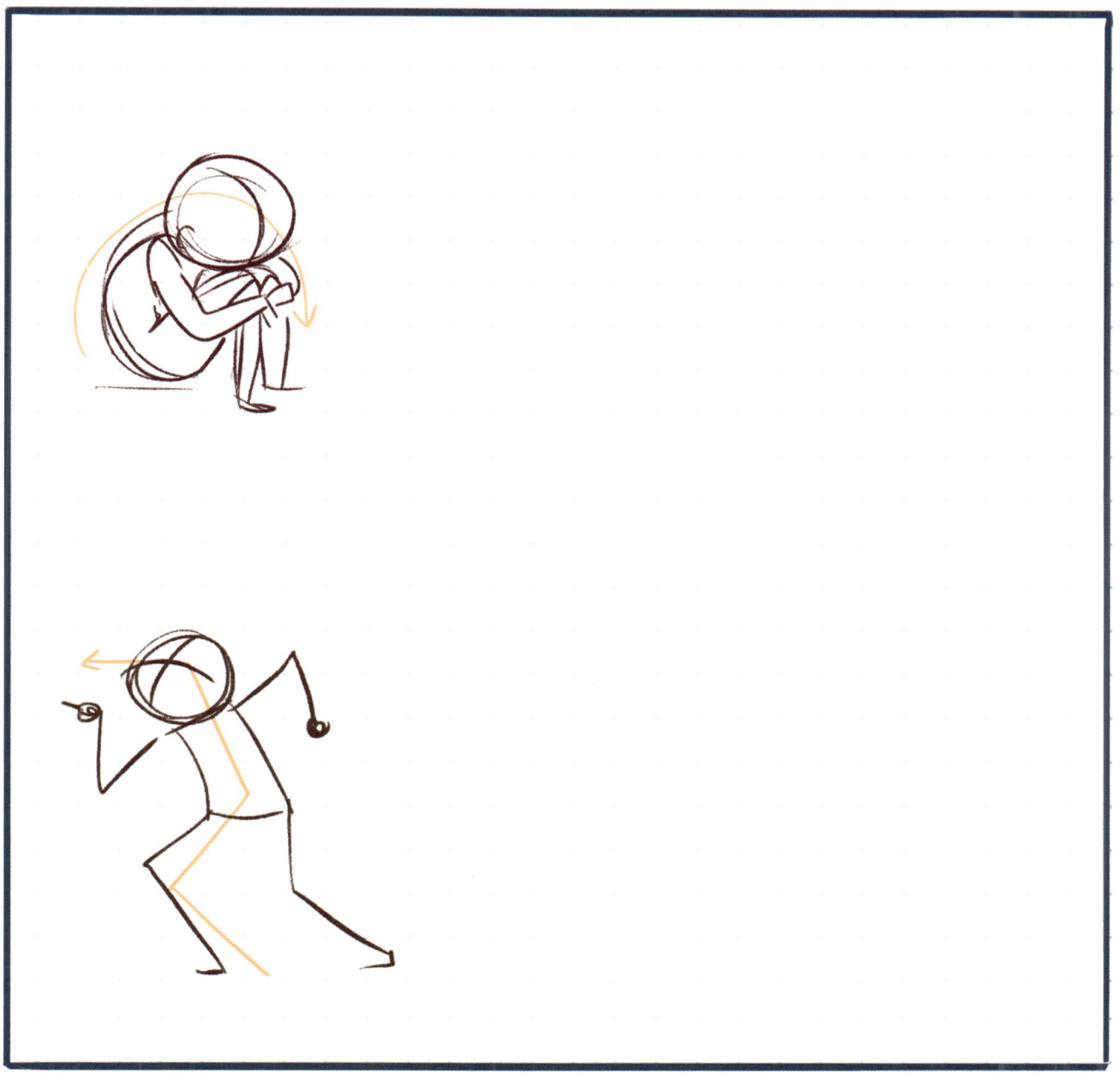

PRACTICE TIME ↘

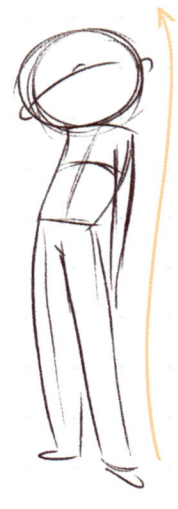

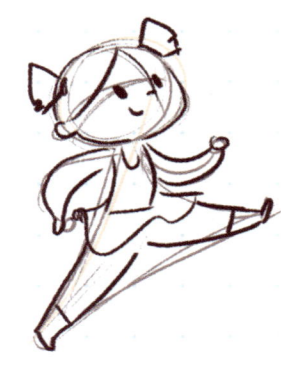

DRAW YOUR OWN POSES.

NOW GO BACK AND GIVE YOUR CHARACTERS PERSONALITY AND ACCESSORIES!

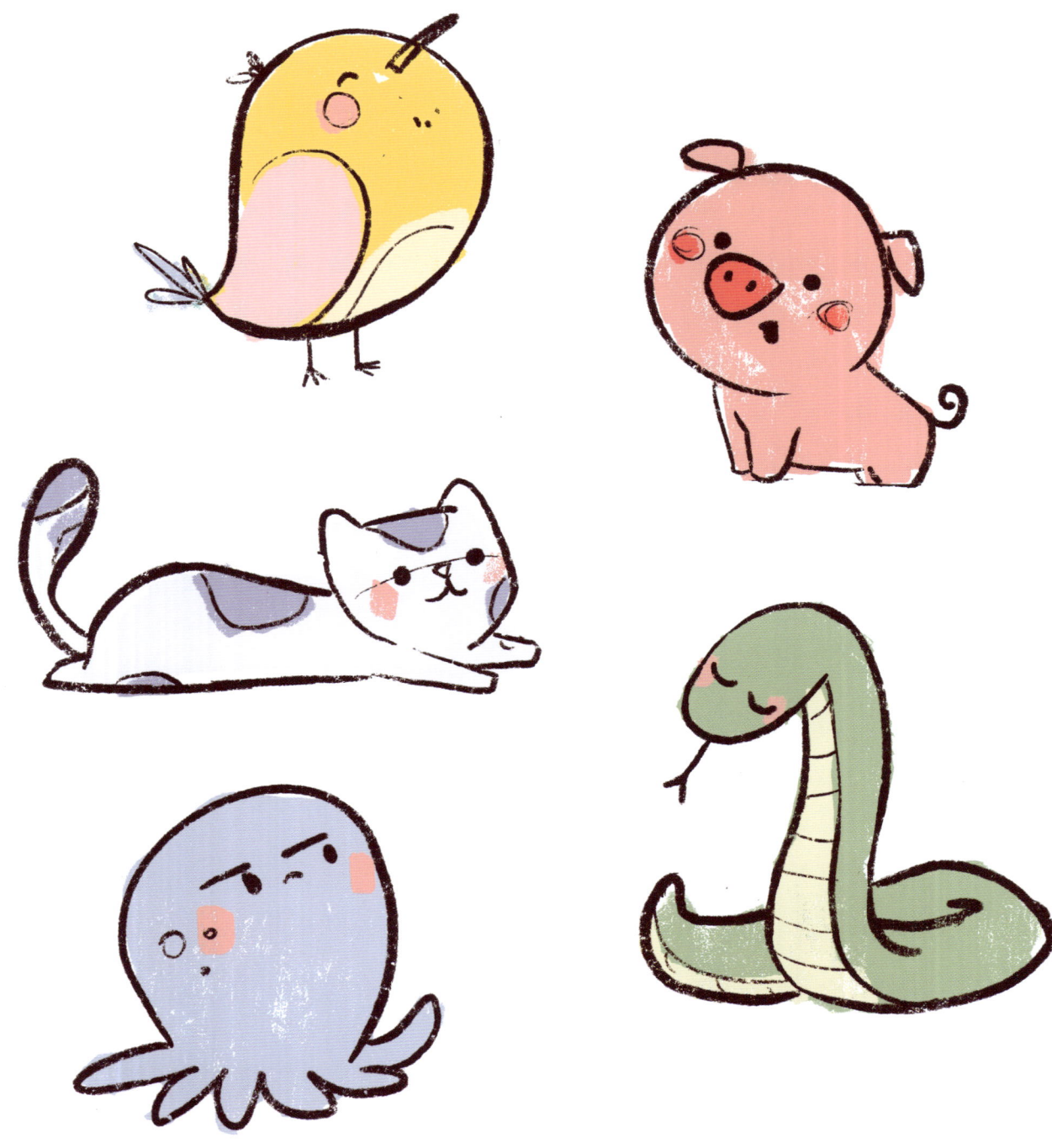

FUN WITH ANIMALS

DRAWING ANIMALS CAN BE EASIER THAN YOU THINK.

The thing that I think is so fun about drawing animals is that there are ways to draw animals without drawing any complex shapes at all! As long as you know what the key features of that animal are you can add it to any shape to make an animal. I'll show you my super easy simple shapes method (try saying that three times fast) for drawing animals. With this you'll be able to draw different animals and different breeds of the same animal. I'll also show you how to add more movement into your animal drawings as well as bit more character and personality.

Let's get to it right meow.

finding the key features

The key to drawing any animal with simple shapes is knowing what the key traits they have. Then as long as you use enough of those you can draw them as silly as you'd like.

WHAT MAKES THEM UNIQUE?

Let's take a snake as an example. A snake is most known for its long slithery body. With just this one trait drawn, most people will guess you've drawn a snake. (Unless they're more of a worm fan.)

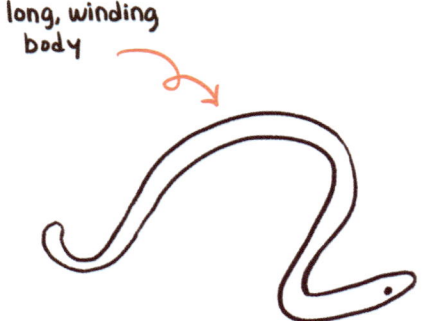

ANYTHING ELSE?

Other traits of a snake are the forked tongue and their scales.

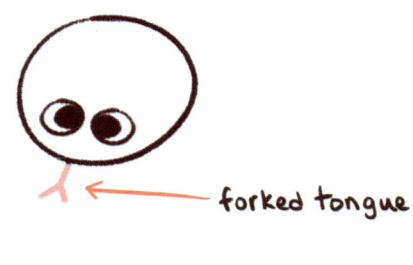

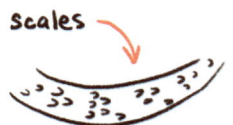

YOU MIGHT ONLY NEED ONE UNIQUE TRAIT

The more traits that you add the more clear and true to life your drawing will be. You might only need one trait for it to make sense.

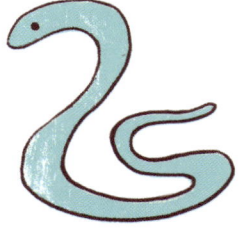
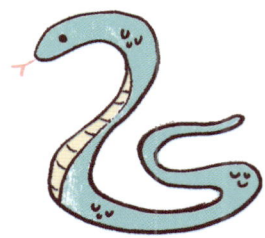

already a snake   nice details

OR YOU'LL NEED SEVERAL

If you don't use the main key trait of your animal (in this case the long slithery body), you'll need to use more of its other traits for clarity.

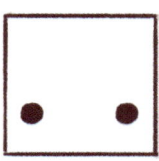
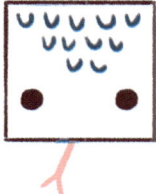

definitely not a snake   it's a snake!

≳tip!≲

Once you've added enough key features to make your drawing look like the animal it's supposed to be, you can add any other features you want—like tiny little legs!

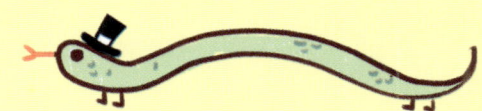

let's draw some animals

Now that you know how to look for other key traits, let's look at how we can apply that to lots of different kinds of animals.

FUN-SHAPED FISHIES

For example, you can use any shape you'd like to make some fishies! Fish have scales, fins, and round beady eyes for their key traits.

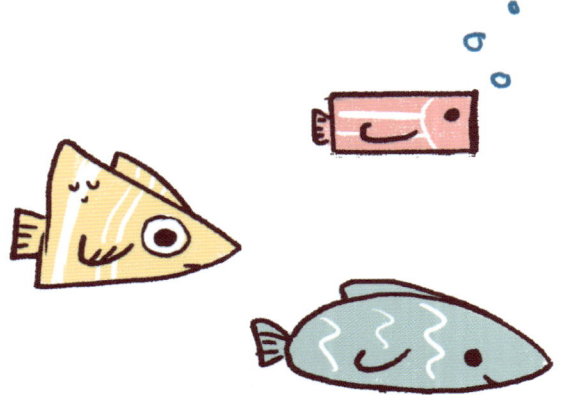

PLAY WITH STYLE

If you want to have a more realistic style, you can just use more complicated shapes and extra true-to-life details. Or keep your shapes simple to make cute stuff.

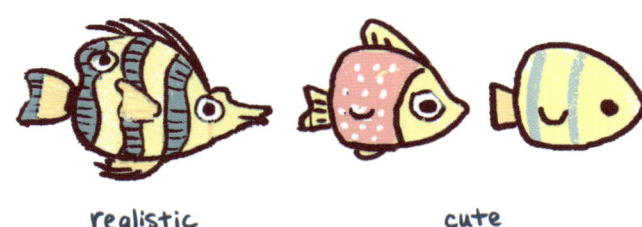

realistic   cute

PICKING BIRDY SHAPES

Here's another example of choosing complex versus simple shapes. Which style do you like most?

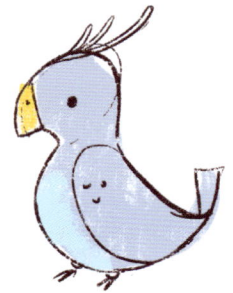 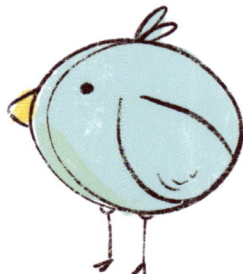

more true to life   using simple shapes

DRAWING SPECIFIC BIRDS

If you use simple shapes, make sure you use other distinct traits for clarity. For example, a goose has a an especially long neck, but if I don't show that I need to make sure the wide orange nose and feet are still included.

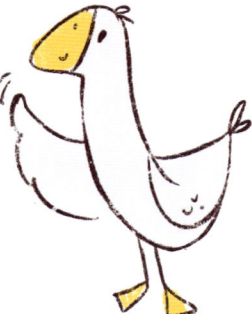 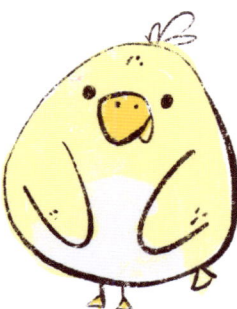

STEP-BY-STEP PUP

By using a tube shape, like we learned in the round shapes chapter, I can create the body and know where the legs should be.

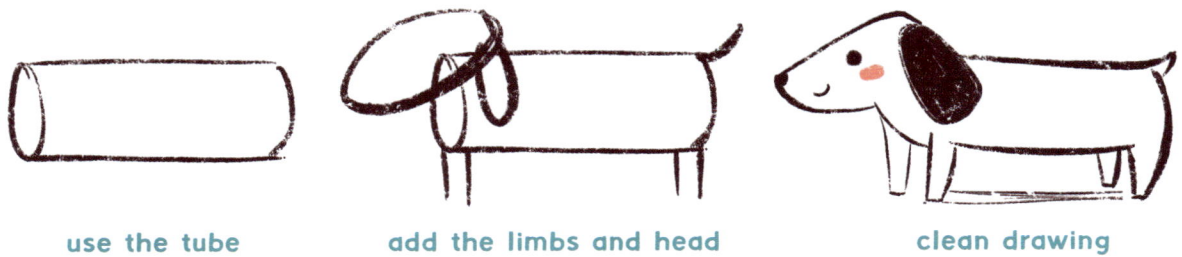

use the tube   add the limbs and head   clean drawing

HAUNCHES

When an animal sits down, it often makes this kind of a squishy shape. It's sorta like if you sat down by squatting with your knees up.

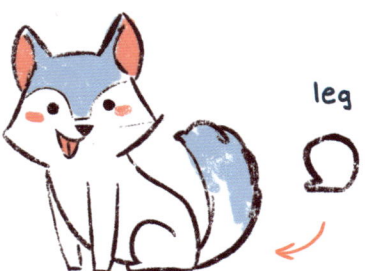

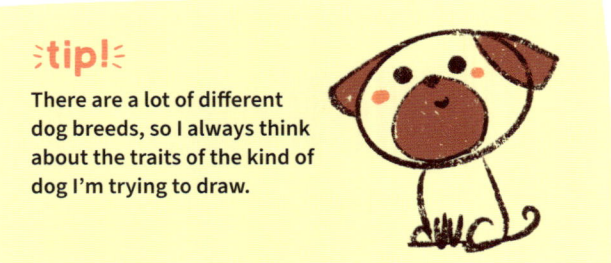

≹tip!≸

There are a lot of different dog breeds, so I always think about the traits of the kind of dog I'm trying to draw.

STRIKE A POSE ON THE CATWALK

The tips you learned in the character chapter about posing apply to animals, too! Try using the line of action to help create interesting poses.

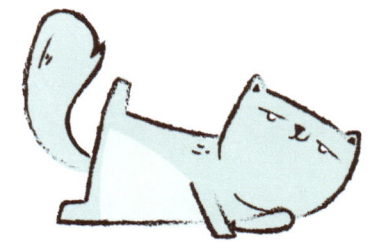
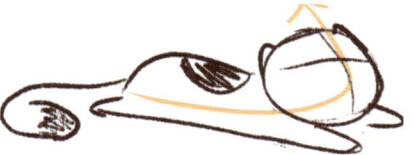

ADD EMOTION AND PROPS, WHY NOT?

Just like our other characters, you can play with different facial expressions and accessories to give your animals fun personalities.

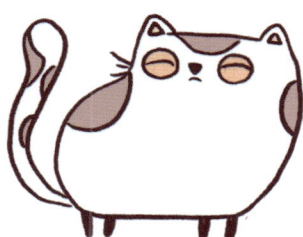
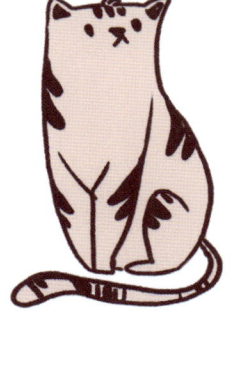
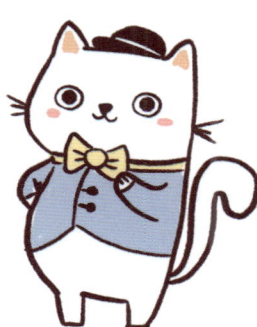

PRACTICE TIME

USE THESE SIMPLE SHAPES TO DRAW SOME FISH.

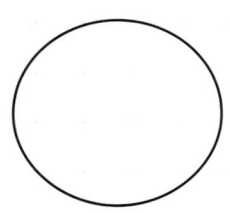
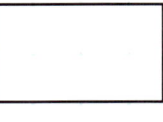
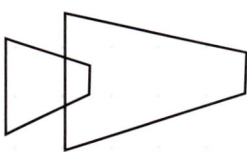

TRY YOUR OWN SHAPES.

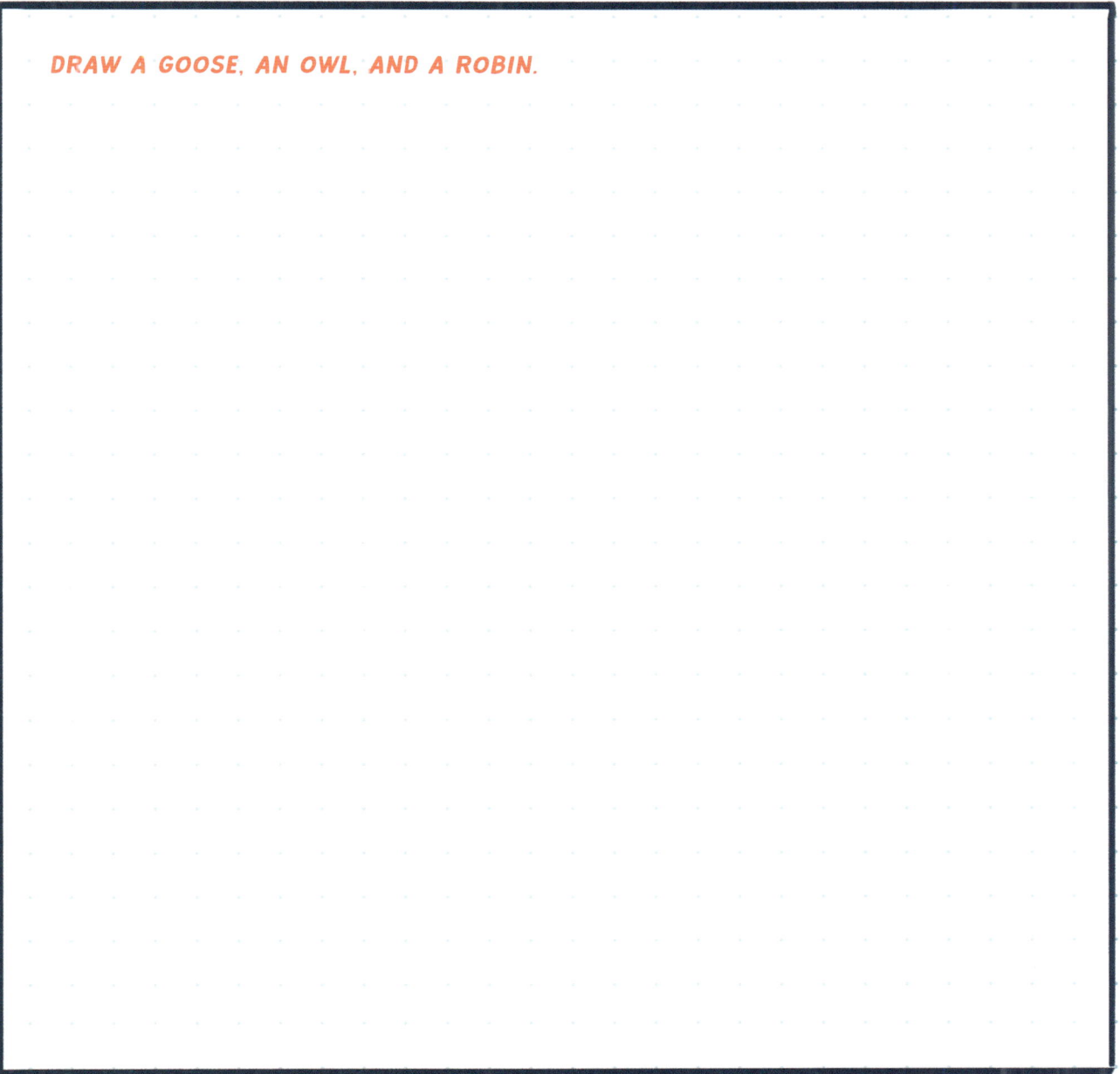

PRACTICE TIME

DRAW SOME DOGS.

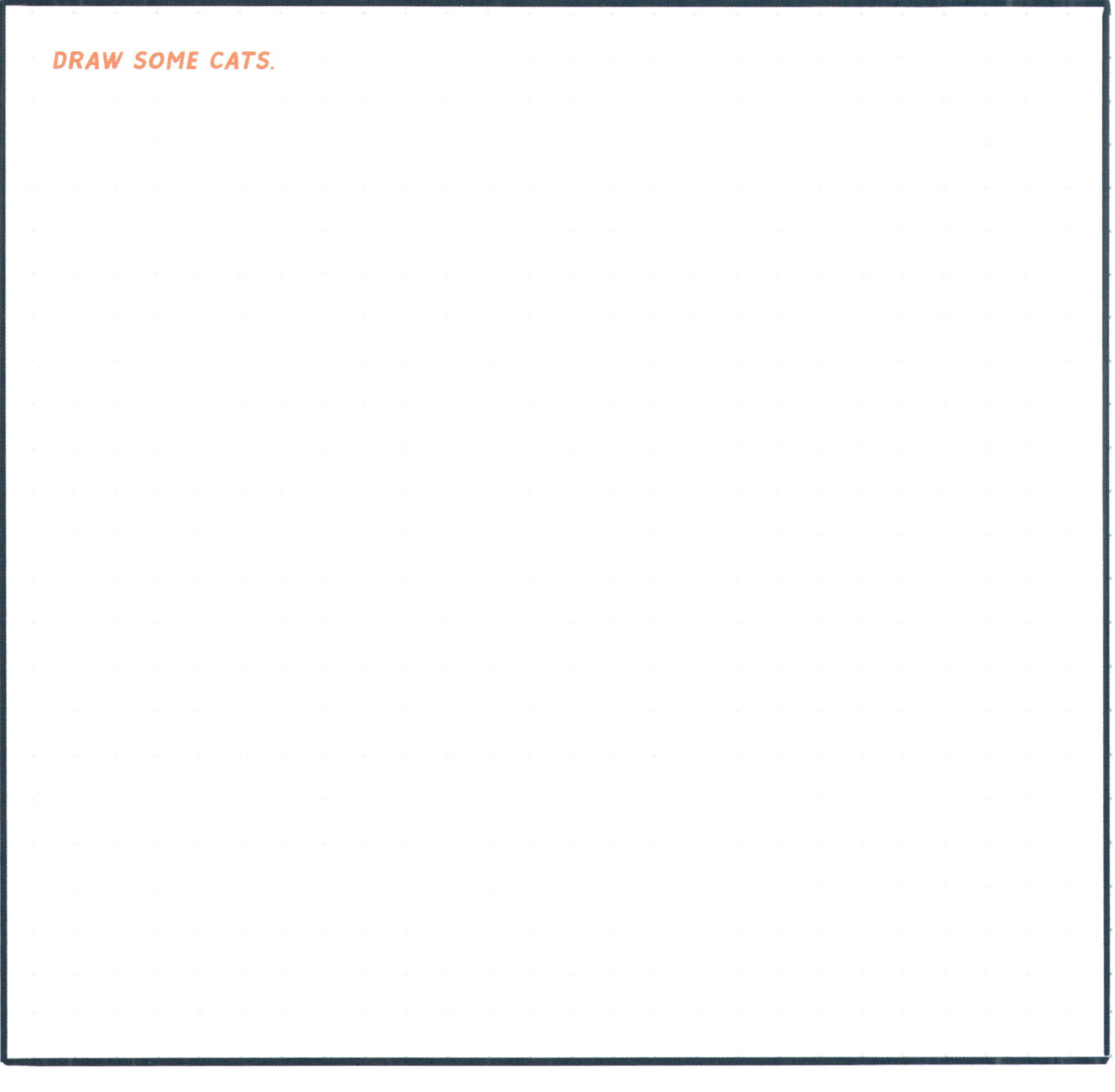

DRAW SOME CATS.

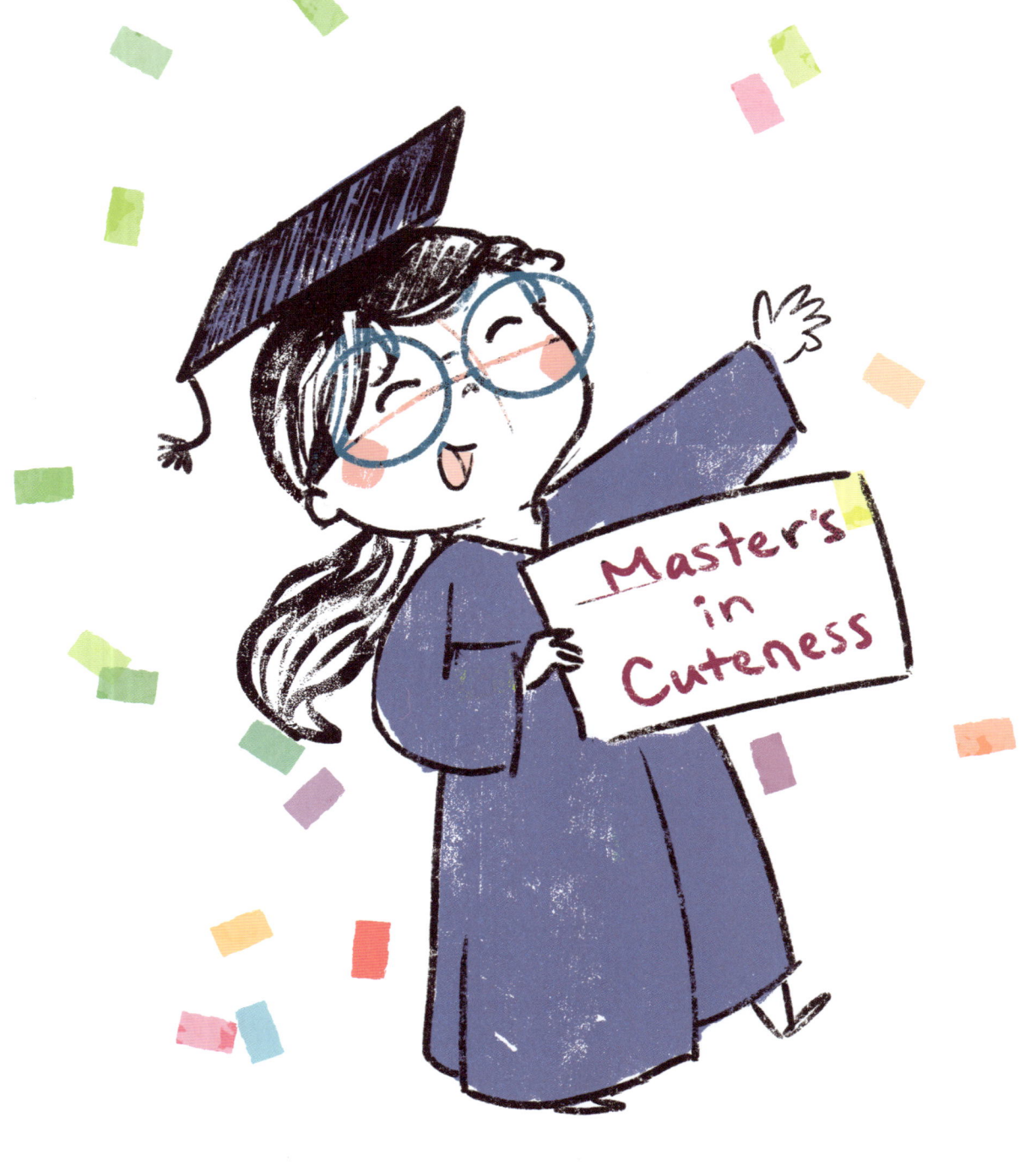

LET'S CELEBRATE!

YOU DID IT!

You made it through my cute beginner drawing book! I hope you were able to take advantage of the practice pages, and if not . . . what are you waiting for?! I have a few more things for you to do before you close this book. I've included a glossary of common terms we use in art and additional resources for you to check out. Most importantly, I want you to get the chance to see how you've grown! So there's just one more page of practice sheets for you to use.

Have fun and keep making cute stuff!

Carlianne

PRACTICE TIME

REDRAW WHATEVER YOU DREW AT THE BEGINNING OF THE BOOK.

IT'S TIME TO SEE HOW MUCH YOU'VE GROWN.

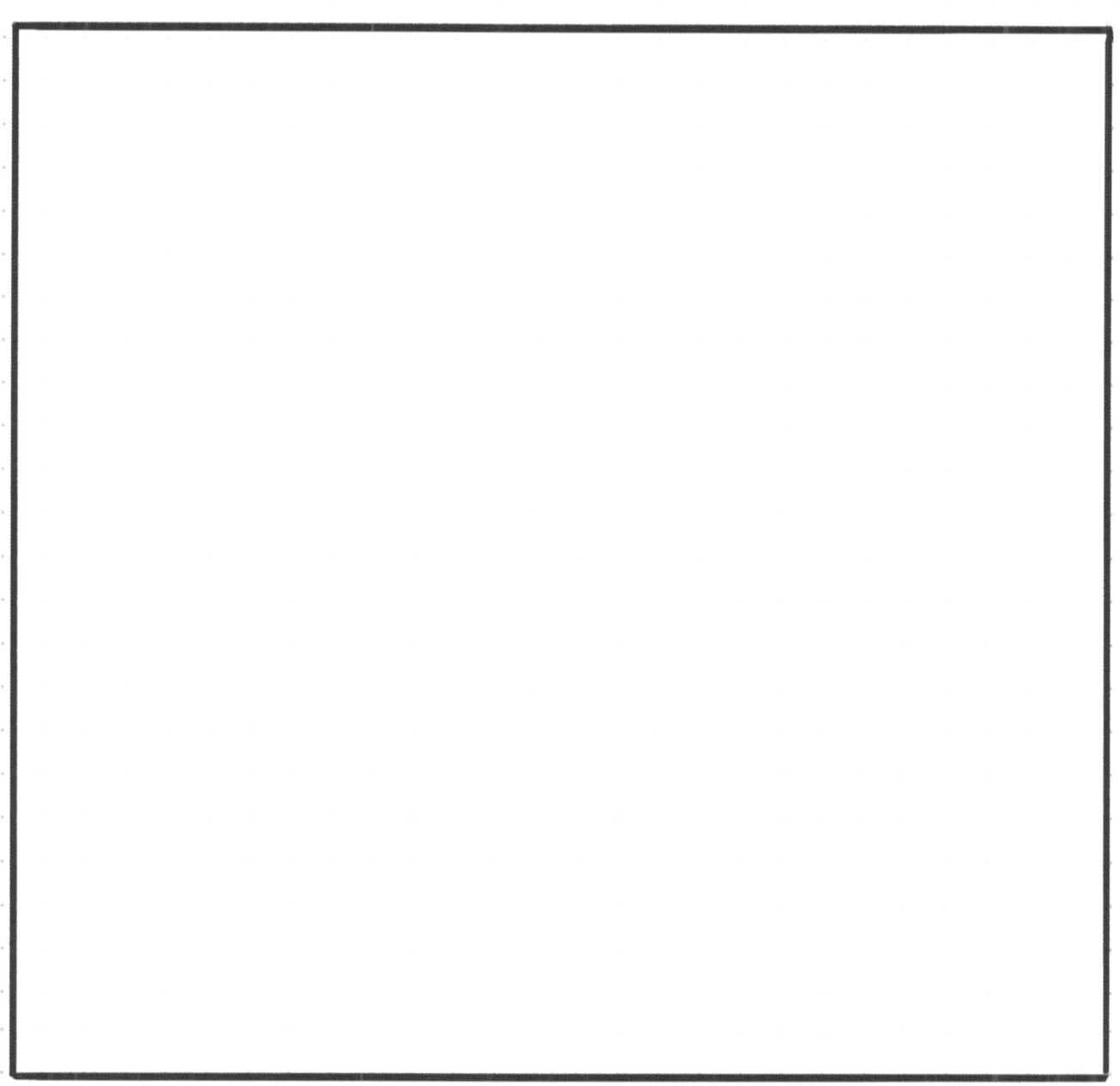

glossary of terms

2D: Having only length and height. There's no depth. Example, a circle or square.

3D: Having length, width, and height. Not flat. Example, a sphere or cube.

BACKGROUND: The area in an environment farthest away from us. See also, *middle ground* and *foreground*.

CAST SHADOW: The shadow created when an object is blocking the light from hitting a second object.

COMPOSITION: The way things are arranged in a picture.

ELLIPSE: A circle that distorts due to perspective.

FORM SHADOW: The shadows that help an object appear to have volume.

FOREGROUND: The area in an environment closest to us. See also, *middle ground* and *background*.

GESTURE DRAWING: Rough sketches used to find the movement and emotion when drawing a character's pose.

ISOMETRIC PERSPECTIVE: A type of perspective that adds depth without distortion. There are no vanishing points used here.

LINE OF ACTION: A single line that shows the overall movement of a pose.

MIDDLE GROUND: The area in an environment between the background and foreground. See also, *background* and *foreground*.

MIDTONE: The color or value right between the light or dark side. This is usually what we think as something's true color.

ONE-POINT PERSPECTIVE: A type of perspective that has one vanishing point.

POSE: Used especially in figure drawing to say how the body is positioned.

THREE-POINT PERSPECTIVE: A type of perspective that has three vanishing points.

THUMBNAIL: A small drawing used for sketching ideas.

TWO-POINT PERSPECTIVE: A type of perspective that has two vanishing points.

VALUE: How light or dark something is.

VANISHING POINT: A point in space used in perspective that lines will all come together at.

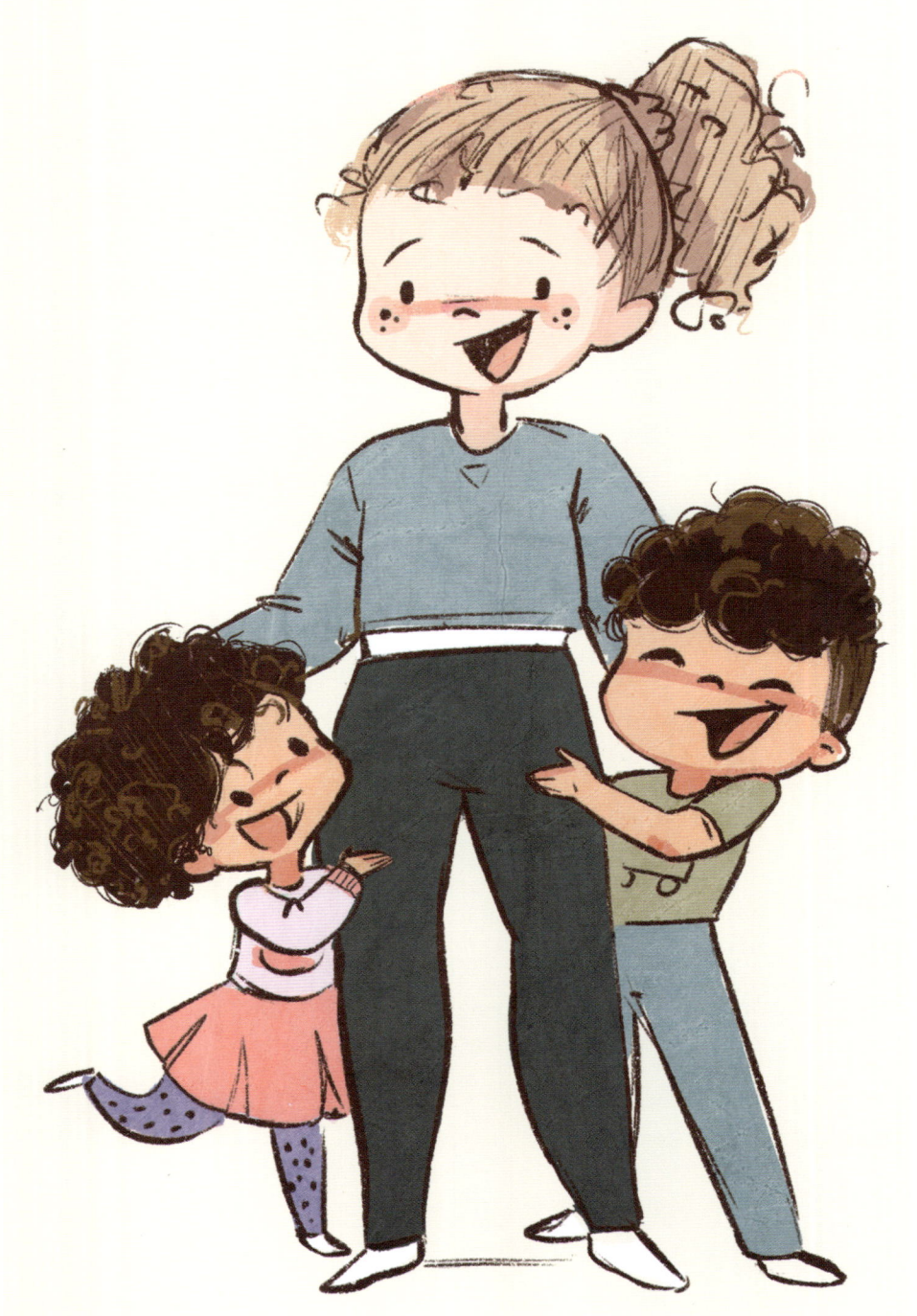

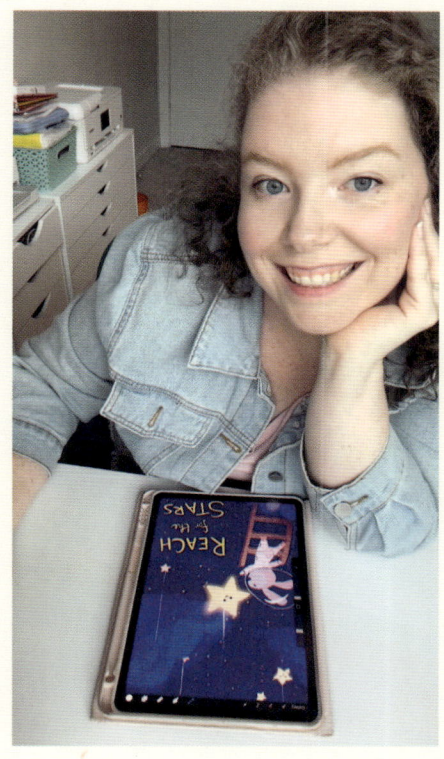

about the author

Carlianne Tipsey is an award-winning children's book illustrator, author, and mentor.

She began her career working in games for Disney Interactive, where she got to draw princesses all day. She later worked as a senior illustrator for a kids' creativity company.

For the last ten years, she has helped mentor her colleagues in illustration and has taught children complex STEM concepts with cute and simple illustrations.

Carlianne is perhaps most well-known on Instagram and YouTube, where she teaches simple, cute art tips to help anyone learn how to draw.

In her free time (what's that?), she enjoys wrangling her two beautiful children and reading them books she has illustrated. When the lights go out, she's back to work creating tutorials to inspire other artists to create their own cute stuff. Because the only thing better than cute art is lots of cute art.

additional resources

**Would you like to learn more from me?
Check out these other great resources**

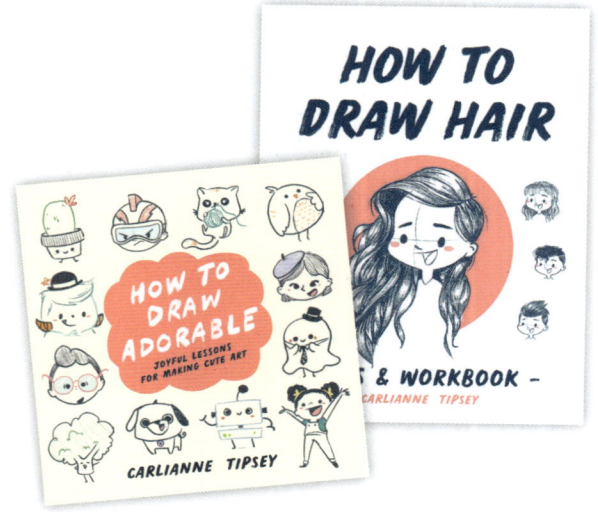

MY OTHER BOOKS

I've written other books, lucky you! I think you'll especially love *How to Draw Adorable: Joyful Lessons in Making Cute Art* available where books are sold. Or check out my other workbooks available at carlianne.com.

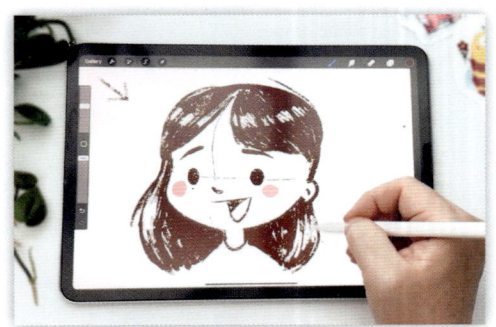

MY COURSES

Would you like to see my tutorials in action? Check out my courses at carlianne.com to watch and learn.

OR FIND ME ON SOCIAL MEDIA AS @CARLIANNECREATES!